Saint Peter

Saint Peter

*Flawed, Forgiven,
and Faithful*

WALKING
with
PETER
from
GALILEE
to
ROME

STEPHEN J. BINZ

LOYOLA PRESS.
A JESUIT MINISTRY
Chicago

LOYOLA PRESS.
A JESUIT MINISTRY

3441 N. Ashland Avenue
Chicago, Illinois 60657
(800) 621-1008
www.loyolapress.com

Scripture quotations contained herein are from the *New Revised Standard Version Bible: Catholic Edition*, copyright © 1993 and 1989 by the Division of Christian Education of the National Council of the Churches of Christ in the U.S.A. Used by permission. All rights reserved.

Cover art credit: Hand: Stocksy/Eduard Bonnin, Keys: Loyola Press, Sleeve: ThinkStock/ iStock/ginosphotos

Interior photos: Stephen J. Binz

ISBN-13: 978-0-8294-4260-1
ISBN-10: 0-8294-4260-X
Library of Congress Control Number: 2015941634

Printed in the United States of America.

15 16 17 18 19 20 Versa 10 9 8 7 6 5 4 3 2 1

Contents

Preface

Theologians describe two different paths to understanding Jesus Christ. The first is called Christology "from above," which begins with Jesus' status as the divine Son of God and then descends to comprehend his human life and ministry in Galilee. The second is Christology "from below," which starts with Jesus the Galilean, in the context of his everyday life and teaching, and then ascends to explore his divine titles and saving power.

One might say that my path in coming to understand Peter has been a kind of "Petrology from above." I first grew to know Peter through his glorious legacy in the city of Rome. His martyrdom and its commemoration pervades the architecture of the most famous church in the world. Only after experiencing Peter as portrayed in the baroque masterworks of the dome and altar of St. Peter's Basilica did I get to know the man of Galilee.

Still later, by coming to know Peter, the fisherman and disciple of Jesus, I began to understand the reasons for the splendors of Christian Rome. Encountering this man of Galilee through the places where he lived with Jesus enabled me to get to know him in a personal and human way. And coming to meet Peter in this way led me to deeper discipleship and a more personal experience of Jesus. I think it will be the same for you. For anyone seeking to walk with Jesus Christ, Peter is like an older brother and a guiding teacher.

Walking with Peter to Jesus

The narrated life of Peter in the New Testament is one of the Bible's most fascinating and inspiring portraits. He was an ordinary Jewish fisherman, but through his experiences with Jesus of Nazareth, he grew into one of the key figures in the history of the world. His richly developed and complex personality in the biblical narratives makes him attractive and accessible to every reader.

In the four Gospels, Peter is clearly the most prominent of Jesus' disciples. He appears in the accounts more frequently than all the other disciples combined. Peter receives special attention in many situations during the life of Jesus, and he often functions as the spokesperson for the other disciples. He is the first called by Jesus and made a fisher of men and women, and in every list of Jesus' twelve disciples, Peter's name appears first. He is the first to profess genuine faith in Jesus, always the first to answer Jesus, and the first apostle that Paul names as witness to Jesus' resurrection.

In the life of the early church, Peter exercises a clear primacy. He preaches the first sermon at Pentecost, converting thousands to belief in Christ. He performs the first recorded miracle in the apostolic church, healing a crippled beggar in the name of Christ. And he is the first to receive a Gentile convert into the community, opening the mission of the church to all people.

Yet, despite this distinctive role of Peter among the disciples, he seems to be a mass of contradictions. He confesses that Jesus is the Son of God, then refuses to accept Jesus' mission as the suffering Messiah. Jesus appoints him as the rock foundation of his church, but Peter shows himself a stumbling stone on Jesus' path to the cross. Peter bravely walks on the water at the direction of Jesus but then fearfully begins to sink.

Peter is bold and cowardly, impulsive and fearful, filled with bravado yet weak, flawed, and sinful. In reading the Gospels, we see a wide range of responses, from foolish bluster to passionate commitment. When Jesus appears in transfigured glory on the mountain, Peter reverently offers to erect tents, but when Jesus asks him to watch with him in his grief in Gethsemane, Peter promptly falls asleep. He promises to lay down his life for Jesus, but that same night he denies three times that he ever knew him. In the early days of the church, Peter risks his reputation to share the gospel with the Gentiles, but later in Antioch he refuses to eat with them and must be reprimanded for this by Paul.

I have grown to love Peter because he is such a thoroughly human character. He certainly has many strengths, but time and again he displays his weaknesses. He frequently demonstrates genuine emotions. We witness him weeping in anguish after denying his master. Then he also shows himself as a deliriously happy fisherman when he jumps into the water and swims as fast as he can to meet his risen Lord on the shore.

Peter never tries to minimize, justify, or rationalize his own mistakes, but he honestly confesses his sins and failings. Although he often fails to live up to his calling, because of his humility and repentance he learns and grows in discipleship through his failures. That's what I admire about him. I too find my life to be a mass of contradictions. And often I try to justify my failures, to play down my blunders. But Peter, like an older brother, points out the way to personal growth.

Most of all, the Gospel writers demonstrate that Peter's own merit and accomplishments do not create his heroic character. Rather, Peter is defined in Christian history by what the love of Jesus wrought in him. Peter challenges me, and he can challenge you, to confront the truth of our own brokenness so that God's grace can fashion us into the disciples Jesus calls us to be.

1

The Glorious Legacy of Peter the Apostle and Martyr

I will always remember my first view of St. Peter's Basilica. I boarded the city bus from the western outskirts of Rome where I was living and disembarked at a stop near the church. I turned the corner and there it was, reaching out its colonnaded arms to welcome and embrace me. I walked up the Via della Conciliazione, the broad avenue leading from the Tiber River to Piazza San Pietro, the famous façade growing ever larger as I approached. I was checking off the premier item on my bucket list before I was twenty years old.

I was a college sophomore, spending the spring semester of 1975 on the Rome campus of the University of Dallas. UD is a Catholic liberal arts institution known for its core curriculum of great books of literature and philosophy. That semester we read Virgil's *Aeneid*, Dante's *Divine Comedy*, and Augustine's *Confessions*, among other foundational works of classical and Christian culture. I had taken two semesters of History of Art and Architecture my freshman year, and now I was ready to see these works firsthand. We had class three or four days a week, then every weekend and on our long spring break we'd take our backpack, Eurail pass, and *Europe on $10 a Day* guidebook to explore the world.

But my first stop, the morning after we arrived in Rome, was the visible center of my Catholic faith. No other church has such a magnificent approach. As an eager nineteen-year-old, I first noticed the tall obelisk dominating the outdoor plaza. I discovered that the massive structure, made from a single block of red granite and weighing 330 tons, was brought from Egypt by the Roman emperor to be placed in the nearby Circus of Nero. It was here in this circus that Peter the Apostle was tortured and died as a martyr, somewhere between AD 64 and 68. Peter certainly viewed this obelisk during the final minutes of his life; it formed one of his last conscious impressions before his agonizing death.

The original placement of the obelisk would have been at the center of the circus, a long track for horse and chariot races with bleachers that could accommodate thousands of spectators. Located on what was known in the days of the empire as Vatican Hill, the circus was adjacent to a Roman cemetery, where Peter was buried after his execution. In the sixteenth century the obelisk was moved from its original location just to the left of the present basilica to its present spot. It remains here as a "witness" to Peter's martyrdom.

Originally inscribed to "Divine Augustus" and "Divine Tiberius," the obelisk today stands dedicated to the Holy Cross with the Latin inscription: *Christus Vincit, Christus Regnat, Christus Imperat. Christus ab omni malo plebem suam defendat.* ("Christ conquers, Christ reigns, Christ rules. May Christ defend his people from all evil.") In Egypt the structure stood as a solar symbol, representing the flow of vital energy between heaven and earth. It still functions as a sun dial and is topped by a bronze cross containing a fragment of the true Cross from Jerusalem. This ancient timepiece of the Egyptian gods now declares the saving power of the cross of Jesus, to which Peter bore witness in the capital of the empire at the end of his life.

My youthful wonder was drawn to the 300 columns, forming two curved arcs and extending four rows deep from each side of the basilica. With guidebook in hand, I soon found the two porphyry discs in the pavement between the obelisk and the two fountains on each side of it. Standing on these two spots—the two foci of the ellipse—one experiences the illusion that each of the colonnades has only a single row of columns. The colonnades form a permeable boundary for visitors and worshipers so that they feel welcomed and embraced.

One hundred and forty statues stand atop the colonnades, representing martyrs throughout the centuries, founders of religious orders, and male and female heroes through the ages. They stand as witness to the power of faith to transform lives, and they stand in solidarity with the crowds of believers and seekers alike who enter the sacred ground. For the pilgrims who enter to celebrate the feasts of the church, to participate in the weekly audience with the pope, or to receive his Sunday blessing, the saints are reminders that heaven and earth are united as we do these things in unity with Jesus Christ. The combined effect of the pillars and their saints forms one of the world's great public spaces.

Although I would return to this place many times in later years, I will always cherish my initial impressions—the feelings that Gian Lorenzo Bernini intended to evoke as he designed the piazza, its columns, and its saints. I was facing something far more global and inclusive than I had yet experienced in my young life. This space had witnessed two millennia of Christian history and in that universal Jubilee Year of 1975, called by Pope Paul VI, I encountered tourists, students, and pilgrims from every continent on earth.

Popes in the Line of Peter

The evening that Pope Francis was elected, I had just arrived in Jerusalem for a month of research, staying at the Jesuit-run Pontifical Biblical Institute where I had lived as a graduate student many years before. I was now fifty-seven years old. As I joined the community to watch the news from Rome, the announcement of the first pope from the Society of Jesus stirred the Jesuit priests and brothers around me with joy. Although I am not a Jesuit, I felt a deep sense of spiritual kinship after being formed in Ignatian spirituality during my six years of Jesuit education in Rome and Jerusalem.

The focus of the world was on St. Peter's Piazza, that sacred space that had enveloped me since my young adulthood. As thousands of people gathered, along with millions throughout the world via the marvels of international broadcasting, Pope Francis was presented as the 266th successor to St. Peter. The newly elected Francis said, "The duty of the conclave was to appoint a bishop of Rome. And it seems to me that my brother cardinals went to fetch him at the end of the world. But here I am."

My mind wandered back to 1977, when I had again journeyed to Rome for graduate studies at the Jesuit Gregorian University. Although I was only twenty-two years old, I came with a firmer purpose than in my college days, and the rich history of the city of Rome became ever more pertinent for the emerging direction of my life.

I was living in Rome during 1978, which has become known as the "Year of the Three Popes." Pope Paul VI was growing frail after guiding the church during the tumultuous years following the Second Vatican Council, and on August 6 his death was announced to the world. I attended his stately funeral in St. Peter's and then experienced the excitement of watching the cardinals come to Rome from around the world to choose a successor.

Albino Luciani was elected on August 26 on only the fourth ballot and took the double name, John Paul I. He wanted to give homage to his two immediate predecessors, Pope John XXIII and Pope Paul VI, and to assure the world that the work of church renewal begun by them would continue under the guiding documents of the council. I was among the throngs held close within the colonnades as we watched the white smoke billow from the Sistine Chapel and heard the first words of the new successor in the line of Peter. But his sudden death thirty-three days later ended the refreshing change that his election represented to many. As still the most recent Italian-born pope, he is remembered as *Il Papa del Sorriso* ("the Smiling Pope"), and several news media dubbed him "the September Pope." His kind personality seemed to bring a warm and gentle touch to the sometimes ostentatious papacy. At his funeral he was aptly described as "a flashing comet who briefly lit up the church."

As a new semester of studies began for me in Rome, I walked to St. Peter's every evening after classes to be a part of the crowd and to feel the electricity that filled the air as the cardinals returned to the city to elect a new pope. The doors of the Sistine Chapel were sealed as the conclave began. The electors were split between two strong Italian candidates: the progressive Cardinal Benelli and the conservative Cardinal Siri. But both faced too much opposition to prevail, and the electors turned to a compromise candidate: the Polish Cardinal Karol Wojtyla.

I have fond memories of that evening. A full moon was shining down upon us as I gathered with a few friends near the obelisk. That ancient Egyptian solar symbol reflecting the light of the bright moon reminded me again that the heavens were pouring down their energies upon the earth that night. As the silvery smoke came forth from the chimney, Pope John Paul II was introduced to the world: *Annuntio vobis gaudium magnum: Habemus papam! Eminentissimum ac reverendissimum dominum, dominum Carolum, sanctæ romanæ Ecclesiæ cardinalem, Wojtyła, qui sibi nomen imposuit Ioannis Pauli.* ("I announce to you a great joy: We have a pope! The most eminent and most reverend Lord, the Lord Charles of the Holy Roman Church, Cardinal Wojtyla, who took the name of John Paul.")

That autumn of the three popes in Rome launched the second-longest papacy in history. John Paul II served as pope throughout my remaining years of study in Rome, which included two more years of theology at the Gregorian University and three more years of specialized biblical studies at the Pontifical Biblical Institute. I often visited the Piazza San Pietro during the following years, bringing guests to see an outdoor papal audience or to experience special liturgies and canonizations.

Pope John Paul II was noted for his multilingual skills. Every Christmas and Easter he would deliver the traditional blessing, *Urbi et Orbi* ("to the City and to the World"), in imitation of the proclamations of the Roman emperors. Located on the central balcony of the basilica at noon, Pope John Paul II extended the joys of Christmas or the blessings of Easter in more than sixty languages.

In May of 1981, I was in the middle of my afternoon jog through the streets of Rome, when I began to hear sirens and then saw helicopters hovering over the city. Returning to my room, I turned on the radio and heard that the pope had been shot during his Wednesday audience in the piazza. I would later learn that four bullets hit the pope, two of them lodging in his lower intestine, the others hitting his left index finger and right arm. Yet he made an astonishing recovery and went on to meet with his assailant in prison and offer his forgiveness. This generous act of forgiveness struck me deeply at the time, and I have continued to explore the theme of mercy and forgiveness as a central impulse of the Christian life. Visitors today can see a small marble plaque in the pavement at the site of the shooting. It bears the pope's coat of arms and the date in Roman numerals: XIII V MCMLXXXI.

Pope John Paul II traveled more than any previous pope, visiting 129 countries during his twenty-seven years of service. He consistently attracted large crowds, some among the largest ever assembled in human history. I saw him in 1993 on one of his visits to the United States. He had come to Denver for World Youth Day. I had just completed writing a series of Bible studies for youth and young adults, so I journeyed to Denver and was stationed in one of the many booths erected in the city to promote various Catholic ministries. Pope John Paul II initiated World Youth Day in 1984, and every two years it is held at some international location. As these events continued to grow in size, the media came to describe Pope John Paul II as a "rock star," due to his magnetic appeal among those who traveled to see him from all over the globe.

Why such international acclaim for the pope? What makes the bishop of Rome such a media sensation? Why have pilgrims traveled to St. Peter's Basilica from throughout the world in every age? To discover the answers to these questions, we must enter the basilica and consider what we discover there.

Centered on the Papal Altar and the Tomb of Peter

Entering the Basilica of St. Peter is an experience vividly written on the mind of nearly every pilgrim. After entering one of the massive bronze doors and standing at the back of the nave, the visitor is washed in architectural imagery highlighting the ancient significance of the place. Sunlight from the windows above shines down in shafts, spotlighting the central structures in burnished bronze and gold.

The shape of the basilica forms a Latin cross, with its elongated nave intersected by two arms or transepts. At the center is the high altar, a single block of marble, where only the pope may celebrate the Mass. Above and around the altar rises the enormous bronze *baldacchino* (canopy), crafted also by Bernini. It is the largest casting of bronze ever made. But the massive weight of the bronze does not dominate the space because its four columns are twisted, spiraling upward with great vitality. The *baldacchino* frames the magnificent display in the apse. Bernini created a large bronze throne, symbolizing the *cathedra* (teaching chair) of Peter. Within this bronze chair is a simple wooden chair on which, according to an ancient tradition, Peter sat and taught the church of Rome. The massive chair of bronze, representing the apostolic authority of Peter, is raised high by colossal bronze statues of four early Doctors of the Church: Saints Ambrose and Augustine signifying the church in the West, and Saints Athanasius and John Chrysostom representing the church in the East. Their lively movement and sweeping robes express the energy and unity of the universal church in its early centuries.

Above the *cathedra*, a fine alabaster window is surrounded by golden clouds and angels flying between rays of light, casting mystical warmth through the basilica with the afternoon sun. The window is divided into twelve sections, in homage to the twelve apostles who carried the gospel throughout the world. And at its center is the luminous dove, expressing the Holy Spirit, who forever guides the church toward its fullness.

High above, on the golden background of the frieze, is the Latin inscription: *O Pastor Ecclesiae, tu omnes Christi pascis agnos et oves.* ("O pastor of the Church, you feed all Christ's lambs and sheep.") Next to it, the same message is also written in Greek. The prayer alludes to the words of the risen Christ to Peter when he meets him on the shores of the Sea of Galilee. After asking Peter three times if he loves him, Jesus commissions him to feed the lambs and sheep of his flock.

This baroque masterpiece pays tribute to the heart of the entire basilica beneath the high altar—the tomb of St. Peter. In front of the altar, a double ramp of stairs descends to a lower chapel. A marble banner leading to this chapel reads: *Sepulcrum Sancti Petri Apostoli* ("The

Tomb of Peter the Apostle"). The entire sunken area is illuminated with one hundred continuously burning oil lamps and is called the Confessio, built to honor Peter's confession of faith that led to his martyrdom.

The center of the Confessio is a niche containing a mosaic of Christ and a bronze urn containing white stoles (palliums) embroidered with black crosses and woven with the wool of lambs. After the appointment of new patriarchs and metropolitans (archbishops), the pope places a pallium on their shoulders. The wool from the lamb becomes a sign of their unity with St. Peter and of their imitation of Christ the Shepherd, who bore the lost sheep around his shoulders.

The level of this chapel is the floor of the earlier Basilica of St. Peter built in the fourth century by Constantine, the first Christian emperor. Although that earlier church was only about half the size of the present basilica, it too was centered on this burial place. But even before the Constantinian church, a shrine was built over the tomb of Peter in the second century to mark the grave and to serve as a place of prayer for Christians in those early decades of the church. When Constantine started to build the old Saint Peter's, he recognized the venerated spot of the apostle's tomb and its shrine, encased it in a box of marble and porphyry, and built the high altar directly above it. However, he filled the remainder of the necropolis (city of the dead) with dirt and covered over the first century tombs buried next to Nero's circus to construct the new church.

Since the time of Constantine, tradition and strong historical evidence have testified to the existence of Peter's tomb directly below the high altar. For this reason, many of the bishops of Rome in the line of Peter have been buried in the crypt around his tomb, and pilgrims from the earliest centuries have traveled here to pray. But only in the 1940s, during the pontificate of Pius XII, did excavations below the basilica begin. A series of mausoleums were unearthed and eventually the tomb of Peter and his remains were discovered. Pope Paul VI announced in 1968 that the remains of St. Peter had been "identified in a way that we can consider convincing" and tours of the underground excavations began in the 1970s.

I have toured this ancient cemetery beneath St. Peter's many times over the years. Each experience is a great thrill. Just stepping into the necropolis means walking along Roman soil from 2000 years ago. Through these ancient streets the Roman disciples of Jesus walked and worshiped with trust in the Spirit and confidence in Christ's resurrection. Yet I can imagine the grief of those Roman Christians who laid Peter in his tomb. He would have been buried secretly during those times of persecution, but with sufficient clues to indicate to Christian pilgrims the location of his tomb. Perhaps the grave was used as a site for small gatherings of believers in the dead of night. Maybe during calmer times, the simple shrine of Peter was the site for Christian baptisms, Eucharistic assemblies, and funerals. The remains of St. Peter would have been among the most jealously guarded relics of the ancient church.

Today, these bones of Peter are the hidden treasure for which the whole structure stands.

Buried underneath the world's most famous church, more valuable than all the precious metals and priceless artwork above, lies the tomb of Peter from Galilee who was called by Jesus to follow in his way.

Climbing the Great Dome

The dome of St. Peter's Basilica, the *cupola* or *cupolone* (big dome) as the people of Rome often call it, is a strong and unforgettable image rising from the panorama of the city. This was the intention of Michelangelo, who supervised his masterpiece until his death. He designed it to provide the heartening landmark for pilgrims coming for the great Jubilee in 1600. And for all seekers thereafter it represents a guiding beacon to the holy shrine of the apostle.

Ascending this *cupolone* is a thrill for any visitor. The first stop on the climb is the circular gallery around the interior drum of the dome. At this level we are about halfway between the floor and the top of the dome. This is my favorite view of the basilica interior. Here the decorative elements of the dome can be seen in great detail.

Immediately above the gallery are sixteen windows designed by Michelangelo to form the shafts of light entering the basilica from different directions. And above these windows the dome begins, divided by ribs into sixteen segments. The images that form the first tier around the dome are sixteen busts of popes buried in the basilica. Above them are images of the apostles, other figures from the Gospels, and angels guarding the tomb of Peter.

Circling the drum and immediately below the gallery, in golden capital letters two meters (6.6 feet) tall, are the solemn words of Jesus spoken to Peter: *TV ES PETRVS ET SVPER HANC PETRAM AEDIFICABO ECCLESIAM MEAM. TIBI DABO CLAVES REGNI CAELORVM.* ("You are Peter, and on this rock I will build my church. I will give you the keys of the kingdom of heaven.") There is no mistaking the magnitude of these words as they form the foundation supporting the massive dome.

At the top of the four piers that support the drum and its dome are colossal mosaic medallions of the four evangelists: Matthew with the angel, Mark with the lion, Luke with the ox, and John with the eagle. The quill pen of Mark alone is over nine feet in length.

Every time I view the basilica from this vantage point, I am astonished by its vast dimensions. Walking into the church from below, the structure does not look so overpowering because all the elements are so perfectly balanced. But here above it all, the immensity becomes clear, especially when I see tiny people walking below, dwarfed by the scale of everything around them.

Continuing the dome ascent, the visitor enters a narrow, spiraling staircase between the inner and outer shells of the dome. Each time I climb these stairs, the expedition seems more difficult. At age nineteen, I bounded upward. On later pilgrimages, my legs grew heavier. And on my most recent ascent this year, my back, thighs, and knees ached for the rest of the day.

Exiting toward the outside and a bit dizzy from the spiral climb, the conqueror is rewarded with a magnificent view of the city and its surroundings. Here one can clearly understand the human analogy that Bernini sought to create in his design of the whole. We are at the top of the head looking down. The basilica continues to form the neck and shoulders. And the arms reach out with the colonnades to embrace and welcome pilgrims.

This human likeness is not complete until one considers the pulsating heart that animates the entire complex—the tomb of Peter. Enshrined by some of the greatest artwork ever created, the tomb of the fisherman forms the essential core of the basilica. Yet the bodily remains are not as important as the spirit of Peter and his continuing ministry that enlivens the church left by Jesus, its founder.

Building Bridges between Jesus and the World

Exploring the monuments and churches of Rome today, it would be difficult to miss the words *Pontifex Maximus* ("the Great Bridge Builder") engraved in many places as a title for the bishop of Rome. The chief pontiff was originally a title given to the high priest of pagan Rome, the one responsible for the religious rituals of the city. By regulating the system of sacrifices, consecrating temples, executing religious law, and administering the calendar, the chief pontiff formed the bridge between the gods and the people. Beginning with Augustus, the emperor took the title of Pontifex Maximus. Presiding at religious ceremonies and directing imperial authority and power, he was seen as the one building bridges both to the gods and to the far reaches of the empire. In the fifth century, this title was bestowed on the bishop of Rome. But it was not until the fifteenth century, when the Renaissance stirred up new interest in ancient Rome, that Pontifex Maximus became a regular title of honor for popes, appearing on buildings, monuments, and coins.

Despite its grandiose air, the stately title of Pontifex Maximus for the successor to Peter seems to me an appropriate one because Peter himself was a bridge builder. He provided an important link between the earthly ministry of Jesus and the post-Easter church. Forgiven and commissioned by the risen Lord, Peter formed connections between the other apostles and the growing community of Jesus' followers. While the Holy Spirit provided the divine power that formed the church, Peter gave voice to the experience of Pentecost and guaranteed the permanent connection between the gospel of Jesus and the ancient faith of Judaism.

Peter was also a bridge builder among the church's early leadership. After his imprisonment in Jerusalem and his escape, Peter left the city and began his missionary work in other communities. At that time, James became the chief overseer of the Jewish Christians in the Jerusalem church. Meanwhile Paul was witnessing increasing numbers of Gentiles coming into the church in far-flung territories of the Roman Empire. In the ongoing dispute between Jewish and Gentile Christianity, the first major struggle of the infant church, Peter took a centrist position. He helped reconcile the polar positions of James, representing Jewish Christians, and Paul, representing Gentile Christians. While deeply respectful of his Jewish tradition, Peter also encouraged and facilitated the mission of the church reaching out beyond the culture of Judaism.

According to the renowned scholar James D. G. Dunn, Peter did more than any other to hold together the diversity of first-century Christianity. He established the bridge between the early church in Jerusalem and the ever-widening church scattered throughout the empire.[1] In this way, Peter became the focal point of unity for that worldwide community of faith in Jesus Christ that would soon describe itself as the one, holy, catholic, and apostolic church.

Questions for Reflection and Group Discussion

1. When have you made a pilgrimage to a sacred place? What sites stand out in your memory?

2. How does the design of St. Peter's Basilica resemble characteristics of the human body? What effect might this have on a person's experience of the place?

3. How often have you thought about the pope and how that person/office relates to your daily life of faith?

4. What does the stone, bronze, and other art of St. Peter's Basilica express about the enduring legacy of St. Peter in the church?

5. Explain how tradition plays a role in your appreciation of the ancient and global Christian faith.

2

Peter's Call to Follow Jesus in Galilee

Far away from the grandeur of Rome, the region of Galilee is still sustained by the fishermen, farmers, and craftsmen who typified life there in the days of Jesus. Life in Galilee is centered on its large lake, the Sea of Galilee. Fed by springs and runoff from the mountains to its north and east, the sea provides freshwater fishing and leisure to the inhabitants who live around it.

I like to introduce pilgrims to the Sea of Galilee by bringing them up to Mount Arbel, a high cliff that dominates its surroundings. The lookout atop the mountain provides a spectacular panorama in which most of the blue-green water of the sea can be seen. The gorge that divides the surrounding cliffs forms the beautiful Valley of the Doves, a natural access route that Jesus would have traveled from his home in Nazareth to the sea. Just below the sheer face of the mountain are the ruins of ancient Magdala, home of Mary Magdalene. Further northward along the shore is Capernaum and the other villages that formed the heart of Jesus' ministry in Galilee.

The sea was known in the Old Testament as the Sea of Chinnereth because of its harp-like shape. The Gospels also refer to it as the Lake of Gennesaret and the Sea of Tiberias. The sea is about thirteen miles long from north to south and about eight miles across at its widest point. Pilgrims often comment on how the area around the sea is undeveloped, supposing it to be similar to the way it looked in the days of Jesus. In reality, however, the shores of the sea were much more developed in the first century than today. The slopes and heights around the sea today are dotted with ruins, the remnants of booming activity during the Roman era. Their mute testimony gives evidence of a prosperous population in the towns and villages to which Jesus came to proclaim the arrival of God's kingdom.

I love traveling to Galilee in the spring and fall, when the sky is clear and the temperature is moderate. The region is lush with vegetation and rolling hills. The birds of the air and the flowers of the field formed the daily setting in which Jesus taught the good news. Here I can easily imagine Jesus walking along the shoreline, traveling from town to town, and gathering new disciples along the way.

Peter's Call to Discipleship

The Sea of Galilee was thick with fishing boats as Jesus walked along its shore. The fish were caught as fishermen cast nets into the water from the boats. The nets were weighted with lead around their edges, and as they sank, they surrounded the fish, which were then hauled into the boats. While Peter was throwing his net into the sea, Jesus called to him in words that would change his life forever.

> As he walked by the Sea of Galilee, he saw two brothers, Simon, who is called Peter, and Andrew his brother, casting a net into the sea—for they were fishermen. And he said to them, "Follow me, and I will make you fish for people." Immediately they left their nets and followed him. (Matthew 4:18–20)

This account of Peter's vocation emphasizes that he will both follow Jesus and share in his mission. The metaphor of fishing for people is found nowhere else in the ancient world. Jesus must have created it for this occasion. It reflects the seaside location of the calling and the way Jesus tailored his message to his audience. If Jesus had called farmers, perhaps he would have told them they would be planting the seed of the gospel. If his first disciples had been fellow carpenters, he may have described their mission as building the community of faith. Jesus seemed to be using some playful humor to issue this memorable call. He used images of Peter's career to declare his new vocation.

Fishing for men and women was not something Peter was equipped to do. Jesus would make Peter a fisher of people as he learned to follow in Jesus' way and as his life was transformed in the process. Then after the Gospels describe his apprenticeship with Jesus, the rest of the New Testament describes how Peter spread the net of the gospel broadly, drawing many into the kingdom of God.

After issuing the call to Peter and his brother Andrew, Jesus continued walking along the shore and called two other brothers, James and John, who had just finished fishing. They were still in the boat with their father, Zebedee, cleaning and untangling their nets, retying the knots, and replacing fraying rope. I have often seen present-day fishermen casting their nets from their boats and mending their nets after an early morning of fishing. The region still thrives on its fishing industry, as it did in those days.

> As he went from there, he saw two other brothers, James son of Zebedee and his brother John, in the boat with their father Zebedee, mending their nets, and he called them. Immediately they left the boat and their father, and followed him. (Matthew 4:21–22)

The term *disciple* means "one who follows." The disciple walks in the way of Jesus while he leads. The road and the direction are decided by Jesus. At times the way may be broad and pleasant; at other times, narrow and dangerous. Disciples must place great trust in the Master to abandon themselves to his guidance.

The Gospels stress that Jesus takes the initiative in discipleship. He invites men and women to "come and follow." In John's Gospel, Jesus emphasizes that discipleship is a divine choice: "You did not choose me, but I chose you" (John 15:16). Discipleship is not something that anyone can earn or that anyone deserves. It is God's gift. And by responding in faith, a person can accept God's call only in humility and gratitude.

Neither Peter nor any other disciple in the Gospels had in themselves the abilities to follow Jesus and serve the kingdom of God. Even though Peter would become a great leader in the church, he learned that whatever leadership qualities he possessed were acquired through his faithful response to Jesus. Through mistakes and failures, he grew to realize that whatever success he offered to the church was due to God's grace.

In the Gospels every encounter with Jesus that led to discipleship involved leaving behind something significant. Peter and Andrew left their nets. James and John left their boat and their father's business. When Jesus encountered the woman of Samaria and enabled her to envision a new future, she left her water jar and went to the Samaritans of her city, proclaimed the good news, and brought many to Jesus through her testimony. When Jesus was going through Jericho and saw the chief tax collector looking down on him from a sycamore tree, he insisted on staying at his house. And when Zacchaeus opened the door to Jesus, he repented of his dishonesty, gave generously to the poor, and his life began to change.

The fact that new disciples immediately left behind much of their lives to follow Jesus indicates that he must have inspired within them a great confidence. For some of them, what they left behind was a secure living and a predictable life. Others left behind their brokenness, their sin, and their fears. After a person becomes a disciple, life is never the same again. The disciple leaves behind anything that impedes the following. Sometimes being a disciple involves emptying life of what feels secure, for the purpose of filling life with abundance.

Fishing for Men and Women

If Jesus wanted to choose the ideal person to lead his church into the future, where would he look for such a person? We might suppose he could find such a person in Jerusalem, among the priests of the temple or perhaps among the educated and talented nobles of the city. Yet the person Jesus called for the task was not found among the religious leaders or the noble families of the capitol city. Simon Peter was a rugged fisherman, a simple man from the working class of small-town Galilee.

Jesus called ordinary people, not people known for their status, wealth, influence, or social standing. Jesus needed people who would give him themselves. It was not the accomplishments of a person that mattered to Jesus but what he could do with the person.

It seems that the characteristics of good fishermen are also some of the important qualities of good disciples. The patience and perseverance required for fishing must mark the life of disciples because of the frequent discouragement and hardship they encounter. The sense that a good fisherman has for knowing the right moment to drop the net is the kind of sensitivity needed by a seeker of souls, to know the longings and deep needs of people's lives. Those who fish know how to choose the right bait to catch the fish; so too, disciples must be immersed in the real lives of people in order to share the message of hope and love that Jesus offers them.

The invitation of Jesus to "Follow me" and the immediate response of Simon Peter form a model for the kind of choice and reorientation of life that discipleship demands. Jesus' call to Peter implies a personal relationship with Jesus. Jesus wants Peter's life joined to his own, wants Peter to eat and dwell with him, to meet the same people and share their lives.

Of course the circumstances in which that choice is made vary greatly from one individual to another. Many throughout history have been nurtured in faith through the privilege of being raised in a Christian home. Many others have had to struggle with faith through great opposition and ridicule. Some have come to faith through a transforming experience that brought them face-to-face with the urgent need for belief. We can never impose upon anyone the decision to follow Jesus. True conversion is ultimately a thoughtful and conscious decision to make Jesus the foundation of life and to make God's reign first priority.

But the call of Peter emphasizes an even deeper reality about Jesus' call to discipleship. It is ultimately Jesus who chooses and summons those he wants to be his disciples. Although it was usual in Jewish circles for students to seek out and choose a rabbi to follow, Jesus operated differently. The initiative in discipleship always belongs with Jesus. So as much as we may decide to follow Jesus and choose to reorient our lives around him, we must acknowledge, if only in retrospect, that the reverse has been true. In all our searching and choosing, *we* were being sought and chosen. The one we choose is the one who first chose us.

Jesus Teaches from Peter's Boat

Luke's Gospel offers another rendition of Peter's call. The passage clarifies that Jesus and Peter met only after Jesus had acquired wide fame and growing popularity. Here the crowd is pressing in on Jesus and pushing him to the edge of the sea, so Jesus uses the fishing boat of Simon Peter to give himself room to teach the crowds.

> Once while Jesus was standing beside the lake of Gennesaret, and the crowd was pressing in on him to hear the word of God, he saw two boats there at the shore of the lake; the fishermen had gone out of them and were washing their nets. He got into one of the boats,

the one belonging to Simon, and asked him to put out a little way from the shore. Then he sat down and taught the crowds from the boat. (Luke 5:1–3)

Jesus got into the boat of Simon Peter and asked him to row out into the lake. Both Jesus and Peter knew that voices travel well across the water. And here Jesus sat in the boat and taught crowds of people from this floating pulpit.

Just below the Mount of Beatitudes, a hillside area commemorating Jesus' Sermon on the Mount, is a lovely semicircular bay. Here it is believed that Jesus taught on this occasion in Luke 5 and perhaps many others. The area is popularly called Sower's Cove or Bay of the Parables. The slope of the hill forms a natural amphitheater where the acoustic quality is exceptional. Thousands of people could have heard Jesus teach from Peter's boat moored in the bay. Mark's Gospel describes the setting of Jesus' teaching:

> Again he began to teach beside the sea. Such a very large crowd gathered around him that he got into a boat on the sea and sat there, while the whole crowd was beside the sea on the land. He began to teach them many things in parables, and in his teaching he said to them: "Listen! A sower went out to sow. And as he sowed, some seed fell on the path, and the birds came and ate it up. Other seed fell on rocky ground, where it did not have much soil, and it sprang up quickly, since it had no depth of soil. And when the sun rose, it was scorched; and since it had no root, it withered away. Other seed fell among thorns, and the thorns grew up and choked it, and it yielded no grain. Other seed fell into good soil and brought forth grain, growing up and increasing and yielding thirty and sixty and a hundredfold." (Mark 4:1–8)

When I visit this spot, I can easily imagine Jesus sitting in the boat teaching in parables. His confident voice travels over the calm water to the crowd on the shore. But Peter, the boat's steersman, sits near Jesus, seeing the beads of his perspiration, hearing the breath between his sentences, smelling the rugged scent of his cloak after a day of walking along the shore. As Jesus relies on Peter to facilitate, from his fishing vessel, Jesus' first teaching in parables, Peter is becoming Jesus' closest and most trusted companion.

The shore around the Sea of Galilee is not sandy beach; rather, it consists of footpaths, rocky ground, thorn bushes, and also lots of fertile soil. As Jesus told his parable, he didn't need to ask his audience to imagine these elements of the terrain; they were already there. Jesus used the elements of nature that surrounded him to convey his message—seeds, black fertile soil, hungry birds, flowers and crops, and plenty of weeds and thistles. Jesus deeply experienced the environment around him and used the stuff of nature to teach about the new life God was offering.

I wonder what Peter was thinking as he heard Jesus' parable. Although Peter was a fisherman by trade, surely he knew the ways of farming and the prospects associated with sowing seed. In the area directly around the sea, there were plenty of obstacles that prevented seeds from germinating, growing roots, and bearing fruit. But perhaps only after Jesus explained the parable to his closest followers was Peter challenged to ask whether his life was like the trodden path, the rocky ground, or the thorny soil. Or perhaps more profoundly, Peter was able to ask what parts of his own life were receptive to Jesus and his teachings and what parts were closed. Was he concerned yet that the words of Jesus might "wither away" when hardships came?

I'm sure that at this point in his life, Peter feels fairly confident that he can do for Jesus whatever is necessary. But as Peter continues to follow Jesus, he will learn through trial and error that discipleship requires removing obstacles to the growth of God's word within him. Peter is our living model for this growth in discipleship. Life with Jesus means continually seeing the stumbling stones and removing the choking habits that prevent faithful following and deepening growth.

Hauling in the Breaking Nets

The Sea of Galilee yielded a surprising catch in 1986—the hull of a fishing boat old enough to have been sailing the sea at the time of Jesus and Peter. During a severe drought, the water level of the lake reached an unusually low point. Two fishermen discovered the boat preserved in the mud of the lake bed. And after a long unearthing and restoration process, the boat is now on display at a museum near the waters.

Evidence of repeated repairs to the boat showed that it had been used for several decades, perhaps nearly a century. Radiocarbon dating as well as pottery, wood, and nails indicate that the boat was in use in the early first century. The boat is about twenty-seven feet long and seven feet high, enabling it to carry up to fifteen people. Both the fore and aft sections were probably decked in, although the preserved remains do not reach this height. And like all fishing boats of the era, it had a mast for sailing and a rudder for steering. Of course there is no indication that this was the boat of Peter, but it certainly gives us a good idea of the type of boat those fishermen disciples must have used.

When Jesus had finished teaching the crowds from Simon Peter's boat, Luke tells us that Jesus told the boatman to move into the deeper water so that he could cast his nets. Although Peter is skeptical about the prospects for a catch, he obeys Jesus: "If you say so, I will let down the nets." The results, of course, overwhelm the fisherman, the nets, and the boat. Peter must get assistance from other fishermen and their boat to bring in the catch.

> When [Jesus] had finished speaking, he said to Simon, "Put out into the deep water and let down your nets for a catch." Simon answered, "Master, we have worked all night long but have caught nothing. Yet if you say so, I will let down the nets." When they had done this, they caught so many fish that their nets were beginning to break. So they signaled their partners in the other boat to come and help them. And they came and filled both boats, so that they began to

sink. But when Simon Peter saw it, he fell down at Jesus' knees, saying, "Go away from me, Lord, for I am a sinful man!" For he and all who were with him were amazed at the catch of fish that they had taken; and so also were James and John, sons of Zebedee, who were partners with Simon. Then Jesus said to Simon, "Do not be afraid; from now on you will be catching people." When they had brought their boats to shore, they left everything and followed him. (Luke 5:4–11)

The catch of fish is a parable in action. The overwhelming haul of fish was designed not simply to amaze Peter but to teach him. In every parable something surprising—even shocking and incomprehensible—happens. The parable of the sower ends with a hundredfold harvest, a return that even the most optimistic farmer could never expect. This huge catch is beyond anything these fishermen have ever experienced. The teachings of Jesus are difficult to grasp and challenging to accept. He makes them provocative in order to arouse his hearers to an urgent, now-is-the-time response.

I can imagine the scene. The nets are overstuffed with fish, so much so that, despite careful mending, they are about to fray and break. As they are hauled aboard, the boat leans to one side and begins to take on water. As James and John hurry with their boat to help, the men shout for joy after catching nothing all night. The dramatic catch fills Peter with amazement as he begins to learn that trusting in and depending on Jesus provides for abundance.

Peter grasps immediately that this is more than a lesson in fishing. Rather than wondering why he has not known where the fish were, Peter falls down at the knees of Jesus and confesses his sinfulness. He realizes that he is in the presence of one who is not only his Master but also his Lord. Peter thinks that his sin means that Jesus should have nothing to do with him, and he urges Jesus to leave. But Jesus begins to teach him that the realization of his sinfulness is a fundamental ingredient of discipleship. He takes Peter's humble faith and transforms it into a call to serve. The same power that prompted Peter to fall to his knees before Jesus now lifts him into his new life.

Everyone who receives the grace from God to be a follower of Jesus responds differently. Like Peter, we have a natural inclination to resist the invitation, feeling that we are somehow unworthy to be so close to the divine presence. We also feel many of the same fears that caused Peter to resist. We fear intimacy with Jesus, knowing that saying yes would join our lives closely to his. We fear commitment and all it entails, resisting the changes and sacrifices that following the way of Jesus would involve. But Jesus says to us the same words he addressed to Peter: "Do not fear." Jesus chooses those who are humble enough to realize their need to change and those who are fearful enough to realize their need to grow in trust.

Although each Gospel writer describes the call of the disciples in slightly different ways, the message is the same. Jesus issues an invitation to share in an important mission. Peter and the other fishermen leave their nets and their boats to follow Jesus and to proclaim with him the kingdom of God, the reality that God is reigning over the world. This message announced by Jesus and his disciples is called *euangelion*, the "good news." As they seek to follow Jesus daily, his disciples learn how to live the good news of God's reign and how to proclaim it to others.

Of course, the Gospel accounts of the call of Peter and the other disciples speak to all future disciples. The call is not just a helpful spirituality or an invitation to adopt a new system of thought. The good news is about something unprecedented and astounding. It is a call to be part of a revolution. For this reason, the invitation to discipleship has a "grab you by the lapels" quality about it, whether it comes in a fishing boat, at a tax collection booth, at a town well, up in a sycamore tree, or anywhere else. There is something permanently fresh and urgent about the Christian faith. God's offer to forgive us, to make us a new creation, to call us to share in a missionary upheaval, is addressed to us through Jesus the Messiah, who comes to bring among us the long-awaited kingdom of God.

Faith and Doubt on Troubled Waters

One of the great thrills of visiting Galilee is taking a ride in one of the boats that bring pilgrims out on the lake. I've been on these boats many times in varying conditions. Usually the lake is calm, and the boatmen guide the vessel out to the middle of the lake and then turn off the motor. I then invite the pilgrims with me to imagine themselves in the boat with Jesus as I read passages from the Gospels set at the Sea of Galilee.

I was once in one of these boats when an afternoon storm blew up quickly. The position of the lake, below sea level but surrounded by hills, makes it prone to sudden storms. With little warning, the cool air from the heights rushes down the gorges, whipping the tranquil water into treacherous waves. On this occasion, the boatman quickly guided the vessel safely back to harbor.

Such storms are fairly frequent and are a well-known hazard for fishermen, and they must be constantly on the alert. Sometimes the wind drops and the waves subside as quickly as they blew up. But occasionally tempests break over the lake with such high waves that a small fishing boat could hardly survive. Such was the case on at least one occasion when Jesus was in the boat with his disciples.

On that day, when evening had come, [Jesus] said to them, "Let us go across to the other side." And leaving the crowd behind, they took him with them in the boat, just as he was. Other boats were with him. A great windstorm arose, and the waves beat into the boat, so that the boat was already being swamped. But he was in the stern, asleep on the cushion; and they woke him up and said to him, "Teacher, do you not care that we are perishing?" He woke up and rebuked the wind, and said to the sea, "Peace! Be still!" Then the wind ceased, and there was a dead calm. He said to them, "Why are you afraid? Have you still no faith?" And they were filled with great awe and said to one another, "Who then is this, that even the wind and the sea obey him?" (Mark 4:35–41)

The narrative presents a series of contrasts: the storm-tossed boat and the serene sleep of Jesus; the terror of the disciples and the sovereign authority of Jesus. The unruly sea is an image throughout the Hebrew Scriptures for the forces of evil and chaos. Here Jesus rebukes the wind and orders the sea to be silent with the same commands he gives to demons in other Gospel scenes. Jesus controls the sea and calms the storm with his word, showing his disciples that all destructive powers are no match for his authority.

Jesus continues to teach his followers how to trust. Jesus' challenging questions, "Why are you afraid? Have you still no faith?" invite all disciples to cast away their doubts and to put their hope in him. The passage ends with the question of the astonished disciples: "Who then is this, that even the wind and the sea obey him?" The Gospel writer intends for his readers to ask the same question, as the overarching story of the many Gospel narratives continues to reveal the true identity of Jesus.

The boat became a very early symbol for the church in Christian art. The church, like the barque of Peter on the sea, is safely guided by Jesus through the storms of the world. Although Jesus might seem to be asleep and seemingly unconcerned about the perils that threaten the church from without and from within, disciples in every age must know that nothing can ultimately harm those who place their trust in him.

On another occasion, Peter and the other disciples were being tossed on the sea and battered by the waves. They were far from the land and were unable to reach the shore because the strong winds were against them. Then, amid the howling wind and the labored breath of the rowers, the disciples saw a singular physical presence shrouded in darkness moving toward them on the sea. Naturally the disciples were terrified by the specter, and they cried out in fear. But Jesus spoke to them and said, "Take heart, it is I; do not be afraid" (Matthew 14:27).

Then Peter issued an audacious request: "Lord, if it is you, command me to come to you on the water." Jesus' response seemed even riskier. He said to Peter, "Come." At Peter's initial call to discipleship, Jesus had commanded him to follow in his way and had given him a share in his own mission. Peter desired to follow in Jesus' steps and to take part in his sovereign mission to rescue those in peril. So at the invitation of Jesus, "Peter got out of the boat, started walking on the water, and came toward Jesus" (Matthew 14:29).

The scene shows us both faith and doubt. Peter walked on the troubled waters as he depended on Jesus, as he trusted him and entrusted control to him. But the wind and waves began to overwhelm Peter, and he began to sink as he took his focus off Jesus. Peter cried out, "Lord, save me!" and the hand of Jesus was immediately there to hold him up.

How far had Peter walked on the water before he began to fail? How deep had he sunk before Jesus reached out his hand? The Gospel writer is not concerned with such details. The important reality is that Peter stepped out in faith and walked on the sea and that Jesus rescued him when Peter was overwhelmed with fear.

As Jesus reached out to catch his sinking disciple, he said, "You of little faith, why did you doubt?" We don't know the tone of voice in which Jesus spoke these words to Peter. Was Jesus exasperated with him? Did he speak with gentle concern? I can imagine Jesus speaking these words with a laugh and with humor in his voice. Why would you doubt that you could walk on water?

The life of Peter with Jesus was a continual pattern of invitation, risk, failure, and rescue. Peter shows us that the best disciples are not those who always succeed. Peter needed to sink in order to take the next step of faith in Jesus. Sometimes the best learning in discipleship is accomplished through failure. When we fail while attempting great things, even when our failures are caused by doubt and fear, we are in fact growing in faith—because faith is not a possession but an activity. It is like a song that disappears when we stop singing. Jesus urges us to grow, to reach, to dare, and to know that no matter what happens, he will be there with us.

This dramatic scene and others in the Gospels challenge us to be open to what seems impossible: walking on water, feeding thousands with a few loaves, rising from the dead, forgiving an enemy, giving precious time to prayer, giving away hard-earned money, standing alone for what is just. All of these seem impossible to fulfill, but at the invitation of Jesus, we can step out in faith and attempt the impossible. When we keep our focus on Jesus, we begin to live in the new world of God's kingdom. As the water-soaked Peter learned, growth in discipleship always begins with a cry for help. And it continues in the boat with Jesus as we learn courage and mastery of fear so that we can go forth in faith knowing that Jesus is with us.

Consuming the Word of God

After bringing pilgrims out on the Sea of Galilee for a morning boat ride and then leading them to see the ancient fishing boat in the shoreline museum, I always enjoy inviting travelers to a fish lunch at one of the nearby restaurants. The type of fish served is called *musht*, which means "comb" in Arabic, describing the fish's spiny dorsal fin. It was the most popular fish in the first century and still is today. Scientifically named *Tilapia Galilaea*, the fish is popularly called St. Peter's fish. Its flat shape makes this fish ideal for the frying pan, after which it is served whole at the table.

Sharing a meal of St. Peter's fish always makes me think of the meals Jesus ate with his disciples, many of which must have featured this fish from the sea. At the time of Jesus, meals were not only a means of nourishment but also an expression of union with others. Sharing a meal was an intimate encounter, which is why it was so shocking to many that Jesus ate with tax collectors, prostitutes, and public sinners. He was continually extending God's family and seeking to save the lost.

As Peter shared his life with Jesus, he consumed far more than physical food. As Peter listened to Jesus preaching and teaching, he dined at the table of God's word. Peter came to realize that this divine word spoken by Jesus had the potential to nourish his spirit, just as healthful food contained everything necessary to feed and satisfy his bodily hungers.

This understanding of feeding on God's word is vividly expressed by the ancient prophet Ezekiel. In a vision God hands him a scroll and tells him to eat it.

> He said to me, O mortal, eat what is offered to you; eat this scroll, and go, speak to the house of Israel. So I opened my mouth, and he gave me the scroll to eat. He said to me, Mortal, eat this scroll that I give you and fill your stomach with it. Then I ate it; and in my mouth it was as sweet as honey. He said to me: Mortal, go to the house of Israel and speak my very words to them. (Ezekiel 3:1–4)

God placed the inspired word into the prophet so that it could become part of him. God wanted Ezekiel to experience that word with his whole self—body, mind, heart, will, and spirit—so that he could genuinely proclaim that word to others.

In the same way, as we follow Peter's life with Jesus, the fisherman reminds us not only to read Scripture but also to assimilate it. Jesus wants his disciples to experience his teachings deeply so that his word will be digested and nourish their lives. We can let Peter teach us ways to take in the words of Jesus, eat them, chew them, digest them, and get those words flowing through our bloodstream, so to speak. When we "feed" and meditate on God's word in this way, it becomes digested and metabolized into a form we can use for God's reign in the world. As Peter continually discovered, the divine word is transformed through us by God's grace into works of healing, justice, and forgiveness. The sacred text is changed, in the name of Jesus, into cups of cold water for the thirsty, to washing of feet as servants, to visits to the imprisoned, to food for hungry children, to compassion for the immigrant and the outcast. May we, like Peter, consume the word of the Lord.

Questions for Reflection and Group Discussion

1. What characteristics of discipleship in the Gospels help you understand better what it means to follow Jesus?

2. Why do you think it's significant that Jesus called a fisherman to be his first disciple?

3. At what point in your life did you begin to understand your Christian faith as a personal choice to follow Jesus?

4. Choose one of the Gospel scenes with Peter in Galilee and consider the sensation of each of your five senses in the scene. How does this meditation help you enter more personally into the story?

5. Do you find yourself resisting the call of Jesus to discipleship? How can the relationship between Jesus and Peter help you to respond more fully to the call?

3

At Home in the House of Peter

The most fascinating location associated with Peter in Galilee is found amid the ancient settlement of Capernaum. The ruins of the town lie on the northwestern shore of the Sea of Galilee. Here Peter lived with his wife and mother-in-law, and the household probably included children and extended family. Capernaum became the primary base of operations for Jesus' Galilean ministry, and the Gospels indicate that Jesus stayed at Peter's home. Mark describes this site as the "home" of Jesus (Mark 2:1; 3:19). Jesus and his disciples would leave Capernaum on their extended journeys and then return to the village when the missions were complete. Upon their return, Jesus and Peter, and possibly some of the other disciples, would stay at this house, with Peter's wife and mother-in-law offering meals and hospitality for their rest.

No ancient texts prior to the Gospels mention Capernaum, but archaeological excavations have uncovered evidence of first-century dwellings. The town supported a synagogue, and it profited from fishing, as indicated by the many fishhooks and net weights found there. It was a modest Jewish village with about a thousand inhabitants at the time of Jesus. It possessed none of the civic structures associated with the larger cities of the time—no theater, bathhouse, or constructed agora or marketplace. Market days were held in tents or booths on the open unpaved areas along the shore or outside private houses whose owners traded their wares and sold their catches of fish. None of the small streets were paved with stones, and the layout of the town was crooked and curved without centralized planning. As a Jewish town, it contained no statues or imagery.[2]

When I first visited Capernaum in 1980, archaeologists were in the final stages of uncovering the town. Only the ruins of the village and a Franciscan church called the Church of Saint Peter's House were on the property. The most important discovery was a structure identified as the house of Simon Peter. Evidence suggests that it was a simple family home at the time of Jesus. Later in the first century, the walls of the house were plastered, and Christians began inscribing prayers on the walls, indicating that it served as an early house church. Invocations in Aramaic, Hebrew, Greek, Latin, and Syriac indicate that it served as a place of pilgrimage. Egeria, a fourth-century pilgrim, wrote in her travel diary, "In Capernaum a house church was made out of the house of Peter, and its walls still stand today."

In the fifth century, an eight-sided church was built around and over Peter's house. This octagonal style was popular in the Byzantine period and allowed worshipers to form a procession around the holy site. Its ceiling was supported by eight columns and the floors were covered with mosaics. The ceramics discovered at the site indicate a shift from household cooking wares to increasingly fine lamps, plates, and cups, indicating that the Eucharist was celebrated there.

As I gazed into this strange maze of foundations from five centuries, I saw a diagram next to the ruins that divided the findings into three distinct layers: the simple courtyard house from the first century, the house church that developed into a shrine, and the octagonal fifth-century church. There is little doubt, from an archaeological point of view, that this is the house of Peter, the place Jesus called home, and where he worked some of his most significant miracles. More than any other sight in Galilee, this represents for me the historical Jesus.

A House Built on Rock

Houses at the time of Peter consisted of two or three rooms and storage areas around an open courtyard. Rooms were dark with windows set high, designed more for ventilation than scenic views. Most of life in good weather was lived outdoors and in the courtyards shared by extended families. Rooms were used mostly for sleeping, storage, and shelter from the weather. During the cool rainy season, people went indoors for meals and family time.

The floors and walls of Peter's house and those of his neighbors were made of black volcanic rock called basalt, the most common building material of the area. These sturdy supports held up roofs made of beams or branches covered with mud and thatch. When violent storms came off the lake, the stone houses would stand steady, though the roofs demanded frequent replacement.

The entrance to these houses often consisted of a hewn threshold and doorjamb holding a wooden door with some type of locking device. The doorways within the house were made of wooden doorframes and usually covered by a simple curtain or straw mat. Most cooking was done in the courtyard. Fragments of clay ovens, grinding stones, and olive presses have been found. Locally made pottery consisted of cooking pots, water jars, mugs, bowls, dishes, and lamps.

The stone house of Peter reminds me of Jesus' teachings about a house built on rock.

> Everyone then who hears these words of mine and acts on them will be like a wise man who built his house on rock. The rain fell, the floods came, and the winds blew and beat on that house, but it did not fall, because it had been founded on rock. (Matthew 7:24–25)

Jesus says that the wise builder uses rock as the foundation of his house. When a house is constructed on rock rather than on shifting sands, it is able to withstand the onslaught of violent weather. The metaphor suggests the importance of building a life based on the words of Jesus and putting those words into action. The Gospel references to the house of Simon Peter and the importance of building on rock form the background for Jesus' later designating Peter (a name which means "rock") as the foundation of his church. He would be the solid base on which Jesus' church would stand, despite all the evil and violent forces aligned against it.

Jesus Heals in the House of Peter

Peter witnessed Jesus proclaiming that "the kingdom of God has come near" (Mark 1:15) through both his teaching and healing. Jesus' teaching describes what the kingdom is like, primarily in parables; by working miracles Jesus personally demonstrates that the kingdom is breaking into the world to bring wholeness and abundant life. In Capernaum we see Jesus ministering first in the synagogue and then in the house of Peter.

All three synoptic Gospels describe the healing of Simon Peter's mother-in-law as one of Jesus' earliest recorded miracles. Mark tell us that Jesus entered "the house of Simon and Andrew" (Mark 1:29); Matthew says he entered "Peter's house" (Matthew 8:14); and Luke says he entered "Simon's house" (Luke 4:38). This house of Simon Peter may have been shared with Andrew's family, or more probably, these two brothers and their families shared a common courtyard with neighboring rooms. Clearly this is the place that Jesus called home when he was ministering in Galilee.

Jesus' movement from the synagogue to the house does not at all express a rejection of the synagogue. Later we see that the Jewish synagogue was central to the early church's life. However, the new young church also modeled its communal life on the household and families. Within the domestic setting they called one another brothers and sisters, and centered their communal life on table fellowship. Because the home was assumed to be the domain of women in ancient culture, the function of women in roles of ministry became more significant there than in the more institutional settings of Judaism.

This family home of Simon Peter was the setting for some of Jesus' most significant actions early in his ministry. Simon's mother-in-law remains anonymous, but, as was customary in the culture, she was identified by her closest male relative. Since she was identified with Peter, it is possible that she had no sons and that her husband had died. And although the text does not explicitly say that she lived in the house, we can assume that she lived with the family of Peter.

Mark's Gospel tells us that Jesus entered the house where Simon's mother-in-law lay in bed with a fever. When the inhabitants of the house told Jesus about her, he "came and took her by the hand and lifted her up," a description that stresses the physical touch of Jesus as a Spirit-empowered healer (Mark 1:31). As Jesus lifted her up, "the fever left her, and she began to serve them." Evil spirits and all powers that impede the fullness of life flee at the touch of Jesus. Luke's Gospel says that Jesus "rebuked the fever" (Luke 4:39), demonstrating the authority of Jesus over all the powers of evil.

Each Gospel account states that Peter's mother-in-law got up and began to serve. On one level of meaning, we can assume that she got up to cook a meal and offer the hospitality she would have offered her guests had she not been ill. The verb here, however, suggests "to serve" or "to minister." It is the same verb Jesus used when he told his followers that he came "not to be served but to serve." Simon's mother-in-law was not only the first woman to be healed by Jesus but is also a model for all people who are lifted up by Jesus for the life of his kingdom, and who respond to this new life by serving in his ministry.

Although Peter's wife is not mentioned in this passage, Paul indicates in his writings that Peter's wife accompanied him in his missionary travels during the period of the early church (1 Corinthians 9:5).

Even though she too remains nameless, her service must have been significant—both during the life of Jesus, when her house became the headquarters for his ministry in Galilee, and also decades later when she and her husband traveled to proclaim the gospel to distant lands.[3]

This house of Peter and his family was the setting for many other miracles of Jesus. After relating the story of the healing of Peter's mother-in-law, Mark's account states this:

> That evening, at sundown, they brought to him all who were sick or possessed with demons. And the whole city was gathered around the door. And he cured many who were sick with various diseases, and cast out many demons. (Mark 1:32–34)

The Gospel notes that the crowds did not bring their sick and possessed to Jesus until sundown. Previously we are told that it was the Sabbath, the day of rest, which extends from sundown on Friday to sundown on Saturday. When the sun sets, the Sabbath prohibitions against traveling and carrying burdens are lifted. So at dusk the people bring all who are in need to Jesus. The description of the crowds—"the whole city was gathered around the door"—indicates the growing reputation of Jesus and the multitude that gathered at the door of Peter's house.

Perhaps bringing them into the house, one by one with their friends and family around them, Jesus cured the sick and possessed. He demonstrated his complete authority over illness and demons, using it to bring health and wholeness to many. This house of Peter must have been a place filled with great joy and gratitude for what God was doing to bring the kingdom near to them.

The Church of St. Peter's House

In 1990 the Franciscans built a church over the ruins of Peter's house. Although some people complain about its rather modernist design, I think it is a brilliant means of preserving the ruins of the first-century house and creating a space for worship. The church is built upon pillars directly over the ruins. In the center of the church, a glass floor allows visitors to look into the excavations below and stand over the place Jesus called home.

Like its fifth-century predecessor, this new church is octagonal in shape. As befitting the location on the shore of the Sea of Galilee, the art on its walls features fish, waves, and fishing nets. Above each of its eight supporting pillars is a wood-carved scene from the life of St. Peter.

I love to bring pilgrims here to celebrate the Eucharist. As we worship, we are able to feel the human life of Jesus as close as anywhere on earth. Standing over the house of Peter—this place where Jesus almost certainly ministered, this place of healing and joy, this house church of the early Christians, this place of pilgrimage for believers through the ages—I rejoice at the rich tradition that binds disciples to Jesus throughout the centuries in this place.

With pilgrims I always choose the Gospel text of the healing of the paralytic. Let us imagine that we are in this Church of St. Peter's House, listening to the proclamation of the Gospel according to Mark.

> When [Jesus] returned to Capernaum after some days, it was reported that he was at home. So many gathered around that there was no longer room for them, not even in front of the door; and he was speaking the word to them. Then some people came, bringing to him a paralyzed man, carried by four of them. And when they could not bring him to Jesus because of the crowd, they removed the roof above him; and after having dug through it, they let down the mat on which the paralytic lay. When Jesus saw their faith, he said to the paralytic, "Son, your sins are forgiven." Now some of the scribes were sitting there, questioning in their hearts, "Why does this fellow speak in this way? It is blasphemy! Who can forgive sins but God alone?" At once Jesus perceived in his spirit that they were

discussing these questions among themselves; and he said to them, "Why do you raise such questions in your hearts? Which is easier, to say to the paralytic, 'Your sins are forgiven,' or to say, 'Stand up and take your mat and walk'? But so that you may know that the Son of Man has authority on earth to forgive sins"—he said to the paralytic—"I say to you, stand up, take your mat and go to your home." And he stood up, and immediately took the mat and went out before all of them; so that they were all amazed and glorified God, saying, "We have never seen anything like this!" (Mark 2:1–12)

When people discovered that Jesus was "at home," word spread quickly and a large crowd gathered in the house. The house was so packed that many remained outside the door of the house as Jesus spoke "the word" to them, the good news of God's kingdom.

The paralyzed man was unable to come to Jesus himself, so he was carried by four faithful friends. Incapable of approaching Jesus in the house because of the impenetrable crowd, the intrepid four took the paralytic up to the roof. Typical of homes at that time, this house of Peter probably had an outside stairway leading to the roof, which was normally a place to relax and get away from the bustle of the streets below. The friends simply dug out a couple of the earth and straw panels of the roof and carefully lowered the paralyzed man with ropes down to the feet of Jesus.

Whenever I am standing in the Church of St. Peter's House, I can easily imagine the four men on the roof. I look down through the glass in the floor and can visualize the paralyzed man at the feet of Jesus. I wonder what the others in the room with Jesus were saying as they saw the clay falling from the ceiling, interrupting Jesus' teaching. I'm sure some complained about the commotion, considering it a disruption of the teachings they were listening to so closely. Others were probably shocked at the destruction of this house as the sun began to stream down from the jagged opening in the roof.

Jesus could have responded in any number of ways to this spectacle. Yet he reacted with total affirmation to this implicit request for healing because "Jesus saw their faith." The faith that Jesus witnessed was not just the trust of the paralytic, but the faithful and fearless deed of the four friends.

The narrative shows us that one of the deepest expressions of friendship is to bring another to Jesus. People are often incapable of coming to Jesus by themselves. Some are afraid, others need encouragement, and some simply don't know how. All of us are paralyzed in some way by the effect of sin. None of us in our own strength and ability can achieve the wholeness for which we long.

Having already demonstrated Jesus' power to heal, the passage leads its readers to a deeper understanding of his authority. Jesus' words to the paralytic, "Son, your sins are forgiven," are not what the man or his friends were expecting to hear. But Jesus, evidently seeing deeply into the man's heart, knows that forgiveness is his greatest need. Sin is an illness more dangerous than physical sickness. Guilt is a paralysis that prevents us from coming to God. For this man, forgiveness was the precondition for his being healed from his enslaving disability.

Of course, the religious authorities quickly confronted Jesus' claim to forgive the man's sins. "Who can forgive sins but God alone?" The scribes assumed that Jesus, by claiming the prerogative of God, was speaking blasphemy—a serious charge punishable by death in Jewish law.

But in response to their suspicions, Jesus asked them, "What is easier, to say to the paralytic, 'Your sins are forgiven,' or to say, 'Stand up and take your mat and walk'?" It might seem easier to speak the words of divine forgiveness, because forgiveness cannot be outwardly displayed; whereas words of healing require an immediate demonstration. So, to prove to them that he had authority to absolve sins, Jesus did what was "harder," as a sign of his power to do what seemed "easier."

Jesus cured the man's paralysis as an outward sign of his authority to forgive sins. The walking paralytic returning home to begin a new life was a visible demonstration that Jesus possessed the divine authority on earth to forgive sins.

Standing in the Church of St. Peter's House, we can imagine the amazement of the crowd as the healed man stands up, takes his mat, and leaves the house. "We have never seen anything like this!" we can say along with that crowd from long ago. Jesus has the same authority over our lives. He wants each of us to receive from him the forgiveness that only God can bring. He wants to heal us and make us whole. He wants us to bring near the kingdom of God. As Jesus lived closely with Peter in his own house, let's welcome Jesus anew into our lives so that he can bring us joy and the fullness of life.

The Synagogue of Capernaum

About the same time as the fifth-century Byzantine church was built over the house of Peter, the Jewish community of Capernaum built a large limestone synagogue only a block away. This synagogue has also been excavated, and today its white stones stand in stark contrast to the dark basalt stones of the town that surrounds it. It contains two rows of columns with ornately decorated capitals. Stone-carved decorations found at the site include the *shofar* (ram's horn), an incense shovel, a menorah (seven-branched lamp), and a representation of the Ark of the Covenant.

The first-century synagogue, frequented by Jesus and his disciples, was made of black basalt stones. The foundation of this structure is presumably found beneath the white limestone of the present ruins. A marker at the site, situated just above the line where the black and white foundations meet, alerts us to the reality of this sacred place—"White Synagogue" built upon the remains of the "Synagogue of Jesus."

Luke's Gospel notes that the first-century synagogue was built by a Roman centurion (Luke 7:5). When his servant was on the verge of death, the centurion sent for Jesus. A man of great trust and humility, he said to Jesus, "Lord, do not trouble yourself, for I am not worthy to have you come under my roof; . . . only speak the word, and let my servant be healed" (Luke 7:6–7). Jesus was amazed at the faith of this Gentile army officer, presented him as a model of faith to his Jewish followers, and healed his servant.

Jesus taught in this very synagogue with an authority that his listeners knew was from God:

> They went to Capernaum; and when the sabbath came, he entered the synagogue and taught. They were astounded at his teaching, for he taught them as one having authority, and not as the scribes. (Mark 1:21–22)

This was the synagogue that Peter and his family attended on the Sabbath. This was the place Peter listened to the Scriptures of Israel proclaimed throughout his life. Here he heard rabbis teach the meaning of these texts and express hope in the coming Messiah. Then Peter met Jesus and listened to him. Jesus' authority as a teacher was like the authority his listeners found in the Torah and the prophets. In this synagogue, Jesus healed a man possessed by an unclean spirit. The unclean spirit convulsed the man and shouted to Jesus, "I know who you are, the Holy One of God" (Mark 1:24). The demon's supernatural power recognized the authority of Jesus as he rebuked and drove out the spirit from the man.

Along with the other Jewish listeners, Peter must have been astounded at the authority expressed in Jesus' verbal and visible proclamations of the kingdom of God:

> They were all amazed, and they kept on asking one another, "What is this? A new teaching—with authority! He commands even the

unclean spirits, and they obey him." At once his fame began to spread throughout the surrounding region of Galilee. (Mark 1:27–28)

The Jewish Faith of Peter

The close proximity of Peter's house to the synagogue in Capernaum reminds us that Peter was a Jew throughout his life, from birth to death. Although he was a follower of Jesus and came to believe that Jesus was Israel's Messiah, he would have understood his faith in Jesus as a completion of his Jewish faith, not as a new religion. Like Jesus his Master and all the other apostles, Peter was a Jew both by blood and in spirit.

Peter must have been born into a Jewish family and circumcised eight days later, binding him to the ancient covenant. Circumcision was an act of separation from the nations and consecration to the God of Israel. At that time he was given his Hebrew name—Simon or Simeon—the name of one of the twelve sons of Jacob, the patriarch of Israel, and a common name for Jews of the time.

Imbued with the Jewish culture and tradition, Simon Peter began his sacred studies in his childhood and became a full member of the people of Israel with an initiation ritual similar to today's Bar Mitzvah. Every morning he recited the *Shema* ("Hear, O Israel"), and throughout his life he studied the Torah and prophets and he sang the psalms of his people. And looking back on his life at a later date, Peter proclaimed that he had always kept the Jewish kosher laws: "I have never eaten anything that is profane or unclean" (Acts 10:14; 11:8).

Peter honored the Sabbath, consecrating the seventh day of the week to God. The liberating Lord gave the people of Israel this gift shortly after he freed them from slavery in Egypt. Rather than doing constant work, God's people were to rest and enjoy the divine gift of leisure at the end of every week. So, when Peter witnessed Jesus' healing of the man with the unclean spirit in the synagogue on the Sabbath, he might have been just as shocked as the religious leaders. But Peter gradually understood why Jesus seemed to prefer healing on the Sabbath. This day was a sacred moment that anticipated the messianic time. The world to come would be one long Sabbath. So Jesus healed on this day, Peter came to understand, to demonstrate that God's kingdom was near, that the long-awaited Day of the Lord had arrived.

Peter would have traveled often throughout his life to Jerusalem and the temple for the three pilgrim feasts: *Pesach* ("Passover"), *Shavuot* ("Weeks"), and *Sukkot* ("Booths" or "Tabernacles"). He also journeyed to Jerusalem with Jesus and the other disciples to participate in sacrifices and liturgical worship in the temple on these feasts. Like all Jews of the time, Peter considered the temple in Jerusalem to be the one place in all the earth to worship God with the prescribed offerings. However, for religious instruction, prayer, and reading of the Scriptures, he and his fellow Jews gathered regularly at their local synagogue.

The Gospel of John informs us that Peter and Andrew were originally from Bethsaida (John 1:44), another location that is being rediscovered archaeologically. Among the many treasures yielded from the ruins is a fisherman's house, identified by stone net weights, an anchor, a fishhook, and even a needle for repairing nets. Like Capernaum, Bethsaida was a fishing village, and possibly a center for drying and salting fish to export. But unlike Capernaum, Bethsaida was a town in which Jews lived together with Gentiles.

This interesting detail of Peter's background means that he would have associated freely with Greek-speaking Gentiles throughout his early life. It should also be noted that fishing was a profitable business in first-century Galilee, especially for those who owned boats and could hire help. These details indicate that Peter was not necessarily the poor, illiterate Jewish fisherman he is often made out to be. It is more likely that Peter was a middle-class entrepreneur. He certainly spoke Aramaic, probably read Hebrew, and quite possibly also spoke and read Greek, the language of trade and commerce at the time. Although born and raised in Bethsaida, Peter lived in Capernaum during the ministry of Jesus. Perhaps he and his family moved there to be closer to the lake. Capernaum was Aramaic-speaking and exclusively Jewish from all that we can tell. Peter's Jewish identity was formed by two different experiences: the nationalistic fervor of faithful Jews in Galilee and the more multicultural articulation of Judaism that he experienced growing up in Bethsaida. This mixed cultural heritage prepared Peter well for his role in the ongoing mission of Jesus and his church. Peter was faithful to his tradition and knew the Hebrew Scriptures well; but he was also equipped with a knowledge of Greek culture and language, which allowed him to imagine the good news of Israel's Messiah reaching out into the world. When Peter was gradually persuaded by his missionary calling after the resurrection of Jesus, he was able to take the first steps that would lead the church from Jerusalem to Antioch and Rome. He would proclaim an international gospel to Jews and Gentiles everywhere.

Peter Refuses to Leave Jesus

In the Gospel of John, a true disciple of Jesus is described as one who believes in him, follows him, and most especially "remains" or "abides" in him. Many come to believe in Jesus and follow him for a time, but only those who continue to follow, remaining through the struggles of discipleship over the long haul, are truly his disciples. Many people believe in Jesus after hearing his words and witnessing his wondrous deeds; yet, an undeveloped faith is often unsure and tentative. Jesus invites such believers to genuine discipleship, saying, "If you continue [remain/abide] in my word, you are truly my disciples" (John 8:31).

This singularly important Greek verb, *meno*, is translated into English in many ways: "to remain, to abide, to continue, or to stay."

Because the teachings of Jesus cannot be embraced quickly or easily, Jesus encourages his emergent believers to live with his word so that his revelation will gradually change the direction and mission of their lives. Believers and followers will truly become disciples as they abide in the word of Jesus, creating space for his word and living with that word so that it transforms their lives.

One of the most significant expressions of Jesus' word in John's Gospel is the "Bread of Life" discourse, which Jesus delivers in the synagogue at Capernaum. Jesus declares that he is the bread of life who satisfies the world's deepest hungers and thirsts. As the religious officials challenge Jesus for declaring himself the bread that came down from heaven, he reiterates in graphic terms that the bread given for the life of the world is his own flesh. The way that disciples will "abide" (*meno*) in him is by eating his flesh and drinking his blood.

> So Jesus said to them, "Very truly, I tell you, unless you eat the flesh of the Son of Man and drink his blood, you have no life in you. Those who eat my flesh and drink my blood have eternal life, and I will raise them up on the last day; for my flesh is true food and my blood is true drink. Those who eat my flesh and drink my blood abide in me, and I in them. Just as the living Father sent me, and I live because of the Father, so whoever eats me will live because of me. This is the bread that came down from heaven, not like that which your ancestors ate, and they died. But the one who eats this bread will live forever." He said these things while he was teaching in the synagogue at Capernaum. (John 6:53–59)

The writer of this Gospel certainly used eucharistic language that would have been meaningful to the church he was addressing; by this time in the young church's history, sacramental practices were firmly in place. Through their celebration of Eucharist, the community of

John's Gospel knew that they would abide in Jesus and he would abide in them. The lifting up of Jesus on the cross is the moment of his total self-gift for the life of the world, when his body is broken and his blood poured out. The eucharistic memorial of his saving death and resurrection offers eternal life in each generation. His disciples abide in him as they worship him in word and sacrament, giving thanks for the gift of eternal life, while eating his flesh and drinking his blood.

Up until this moment in the ministry of Jesus, he had been successful and well received. But here is the turning point in John's presentation of the gospel. Many of his disciples began complaining about what Jesus had taught and they said, "This teaching is difficult; who can accept it?" (John 6:60). They found his teaching difficult and even offensive because it did not conform to their human expectations. So Jesus confirmed that the only ones able to accept his teaching are those who are granted the gift of the Spirit and are drawn to Jesus by the Father.

Peter is held up in John's Gospel as a model disciple. He is one who believes, who follows, and who abides in Jesus. This section of the Gospel concludes with this rich and beautiful scene in the synagogue of Capernaum, the spotlight focused on Peter:

> Because of this many of his disciples turned back and no longer went about with him. So Jesus asked the twelve, "Do you also wish to go away?" Simon Peter answered him, "Lord, to whom can we go? You have the words of eternal life. We have come to believe and know that you are the Holy One of God." (John 6:66–69)

Responding to the question Jesus asked the Twelve, "Do you also wish to go away?" Peter answers on behalf of all the others. His confession of trusting faith affirms that Jesus is the only one to whom they can go to find real and lasting life. They have come to believe that Jesus is the Holy One of God, and, even though they do not completely understand his teachings, they trust him enough to know that their understanding will grow as they remain with him and abide in his word through the struggles of genuine discipleship that lie ahead.

Questions for Reflection and Group Discussion

1. What is the lesson for you in Jesus' instructions about the importance of building on rock? What is its message for your home life, marriage, or ministry?

2. In what ways was the Jewish family and household the model for the early church? How is it important that family homes were the earliest Christian churches?

3. What new understandings did you gain from exploring the healing of the paralytic in the house of Peter?

4. Peter was a Jew from birth to death; how does taking this fact into account help you understand him better?

5. Peter's background from both Bethsaida and Capernaum prepared him for his ministry in the community of disciples and the early church. How has your background prepared you for whatever ministry or service exists in your life today?

4

Peter the Rock Is Given the Keys to God's Kingdom

In one of the climactic passages of the synoptic Gospels, Jesus takes Peter and his disciples northward into the region of Caesarea Philippi. This area is high in both latitude and altitude. Caesarea Philippi was built on the southern slope of Mount Hermon, the highest mountain in the Holy Land. One of the three primary springs that feed the Jordan River is located here. The Hermon River flows through the area and into the Jordan. Today the area is a beautiful nature reserve, a peaceful place with lots of vegetation and flowing water, located in the region called the Golan Heights.

In ancient times the spring flowed through a cave the Greeks dedicated to the deity Pan. The Romans later assigned the district to Herod the Great, who erected a temple to Augustus there, placing the image of the emperor near the altar of Pan. After Herod's death, his son Philip beautified the area and named it Caesarea in honor of the emperor. It became known as Caesarea Philippi ("the Caesar city of Philip") to distinguish it from Caesarea Maritima, a city on the Mediterranean coast.

So in New Testament times, Caearea Philippi was a place to worship Pan and to honor Caesar. It was to this pastoral and pagan setting that Jesus came at the peak of his Galilean ministry. Here Jesus would ask Peter that essential question for all disciples to answer: "Who do you say that I am?" Here also Jesus would name Peter the rock of his church, the sure foundation on which his new community of disciples would be built.

The first few times I visited this place, I couldn't figure out why Jesus would come here with his disciples. It is quite a distance from the Jewish areas of Galilee and it seems quite out of the way from Jesus' usual course near the Sea of Galilee. As I began to bring pilgrimage groups to this place, I enjoyed with them the scenic drive into the heights of the Golan. But when we came to Caesarea Philippi, there was no shrine or chapel, no statue of Peter with his keys. I wasn't able to relate the Gospel texts to the place itself in any meaningful way.

When I asked myself the question, "Why did Jesus come to this place?" I gradually discovered a variety of reasons. Caesarea Philippi was the most pagan place in all of Palestine. Most Jews would avoid it altogether because of its connection with bestiality and fertility rituals associated with the worship of Pan. And nothing could be further from worship of the one God than offering sacrifice to the emperor and calling on him as lord of the world and savior of all. I believe Jesus journeyed here to push the boundaries of his disciples' understanding of the extent of God's saving love.

In contrast to the Greco-Roman religions, whose foremost concern was appeasing the gods by doing whatever ritual actions would gain their favor, the kingdom preached by Jesus involved bringing God's saving presence to those most lost and in need. Jesus showed the way by drawing close to tax collectors and all sorts of public sinners. He reached out to people whom others avoided. He went out of his way to find those most lost and living in darkness.

This seemed to be a reasonable first step in answering my question, "Why did Jesus come to Caesarea Philippi?" However, I later discovered that this was only one of several reasons Jesus brought his disciples to this high and distant place at this defining moment of his ministry. I will reveal to you the other reasons as we explore the Gospel passages associated with this important site.

Who Do You Say That I Am?

Mark structures his Gospel in two large sections. The first half of the book focuses on Jesus teaching the disciples his identity. "Who is Jesus?" is the question that dominates part one of Mark. The second half of the Gospel demonstrates Jesus teaching the way of discipleship. "What does it mean to follow Jesus?" dominates part two. The first half comes to its climax as Jesus is traveling northward with his disciples and asks them an important question:

> Jesus went on with his disciples to the villages of Caesarea Philippi; and on the way he asked his disciples, "Who do people say that I am?" And they answered him, "John the Baptist; and others, Elijah; and still others, one of the prophets." He asked them, "But who do you say that I am?" Peter answered him, "You are the Messiah." And he sternly ordered them not to tell anyone about him. (Mark 8:27–30)

Realizing that many people misunderstood his identity, mistaking him for a prophet, Jesus asked his disciples directly, "But who do you say I am?" This is the central question of the gospel message. The question about who Jesus is leaps off the pages of history and into the heart of every reader of this Gospel.

The first half of Mark's book leads up to this question. Jesus revealed himself as a teacher and healer with divine authority, the bridegroom, the Lord of the Sabbath, the sower of God's word, the great physician, and the shepherd who feeds God's people. Yet he also met with persistent resistance and continual misunderstanding. His teaching in parables and his great deeds both revealed and concealed his true identity. "Who do you say that I am?" must be answered completely by every individual who chooses to be his disciple.

Peter, no longer just the spokesperson for the disciples but responding on his own behalf, answers, "You are the Messiah." His insightful response represents a dramatic breakthrough. He recognizes Jesus as the one through whom God will accomplish all that he promised. Yet while Peter's identification of Jesus is correct, we soon learn that Peter and the others still have a totally inaccurate understanding of what Jesus' identity as the Messiah entails.

After Peter's answer, Jesus ordered his disciples to keep quiet about his identity. This strange warning, which occurs frequently in Mark's Gospel, prevented the disciples from spreading the word about Jesus' messianic identity. Acclaiming Jesus as the Messiah, the king of Israel, would lead the crowds to try to make him their royal leader, and thus bring down the wrath of the Roman authorities.

Rather than allowing his disciples to announce him as Messiah, in the second half of this Gospel Jesus gradually revealed what it means to be the Messiah. It was far different from the common perception of the day—that the Messiah would be a military conqueror who would lead the Jews to freedom from Roman oppression. Rather, his followers would grow to understand that Jesus was a suffering Messiah, the servant of God, whose full identity could be revealed and understood only at the cross.

Who Does Jesus Say That Peter Is?

Taking his lead from Mark's Gospel, Matthew follows a similar structure in his Gospel, with the first half of his Gospel culminating with Jesus' arrival "into the district of Caesarea Philippi." Matthew repeats the question of Jesus, "But who do you say that I am?" Simon Peter's profession of faith is followed by an extended response from Jesus.

Simon Peter answered, "You are the Messiah, the Son of the living God." And Jesus answered him, "Blessed are you, Simon son of Jonah! For flesh and blood has not revealed this to you, but my Father in heaven. And I tell you, you are Peter, and on this rock I will build my church, and the gates of Hades will not prevail against it." (Matthew 16:16–18)

Peter's response expresses a faith that is not possible simply through human insight but only through God's grace. Because Peter has spoken not through human experience but rather through divine revelation, Jesus declares him uniquely blessed.

Now that Simon Peter has announced who Jesus is, Jesus declares who Peter is. Jesus gives Simon the new name, "Peter," which, in effect, bestows upon him a new identity. In the Hebrew Scriptures, God gave new names to those who took on major roles at critical times in God's plan for his people. Abram and Sarai became Abraham and Sarah; Jacob became Israel. In the language of Matthew's Gospel, the Greek name *Petros* creates a wordplay with *petra*, the Greek word for "rock." In Aramaic, however, the language of Jesus and the early church, the saying is more exact: "You are *Kepha*, and on this *kepha* I will build my church." The parallelism makes it clear that Peter himself is the rock, the sturdy foundation upon which Jesus will construct his church.

Jesus has already declared that any wise builder constructs his house on rock (Matthew 7:24–25). With such a solid base, the house will not fall despite the fiercest of storms. Now Jesus announces that he will build his church on the foundation of Peter, "and the gates of Hades will not prevail against it."

The Hebrew word for Hades is *Sheol*, the abode of the dead. It is depicted in Hebrew literature as located in the depths of the earth. In Greek religion, Hades was the place where the souls of the dead arrived, entering through gates kept fast by locks. Thus, "the gates of Hades" represents the powers of the underworld to keep the dead imprisoned in its realm. The powers of death are crushing and terrifying for human beings. Yet Jesus assures Peter that his church will not be overcome by any powers that oppose it. Jesus knew that the Roman Empire would try to crush it through torture and death of its members, but the blood of the martyrs would only strengthen the church's witness.

Why Jesus Came to Caesarea Philippi

As I continue to take pilgrimage groups to Caesarea Philippi, the answer to my question, "Why did Jesus bring Peter and the other disciples to this place?" becomes increasingly apparent. "What do you see here?" I ask the groups. There is no shrine or church for liturgy, no statue of Peter, none of the usual markers for an important gospel site. The most obvious image that dominates the site is a massive wall of rock.

Surely Jesus compared the huge rock at this site with Peter, the foundation of his church. Of course Jesus didn't need to come to this mountain of rock to make his point. Yet, up to this point Jesus had taught about God's kingdom using the images around him: growing seeds, flying birds and blooming flowers, shepherds guiding their sheep, nets full of fish. Jesus didn't need to stretch his listeners' imaginations; these object lessons were present on site. So too, the rock. The parallel is inescapable. Just as the city before them was built on a distinctive massive wall of rock, so Simon was to become the indestructible Rock of Jesus' future church. While Caesarea Philippi was built upon this wall of rock to offer sacrifice to Caesar and the pagan god Pan, Jesus established his church to offer sacrifice and give honor to the one true God, the Father of Jesus Christ.

But there is another sight here that is impossible to miss: the large entrance to a cave. To the pagan mind, the cave created a gate to the underworld. Underground water flowing within a cave was the sure indication that the area served as a path to and from the shadowy world called Hades. This gate of Hades at Caesarea Philippi was believed to be the way for the fertility gods to go to the underworld during the dry season, only to be coaxed out again with fertility rituals when rains were due to come.

The Greek god Pan shared the horns, hindquarters, legs, and hooves of a goat. He was god of shepherd and flocks, of fruitfulness and the season of spring. The worship of Pan simply replaced the cult of the older Canaanite baals of the area. Rebellious kings of Israel had angered God and provoked the wrath of the prophets by allowing the worship of such idols. The temple to Pan was simply a newer incarnation of the human tendency to placate the gods so that they would bring prosperity. The names of the gods changed, but similar rituals show that these religions are really about placating the gods.

Here in this pagan place, Jesus first revealed his desire to establish a church. It would be built on Peter the rock, and the gates of Hades would never prevail against it. As Peter professed, Jesus is the Son of the living God, not the recycled gods of ancient myths. His church would not be concerned with winning divine favors through animal sacrifices or sexual rituals. Rather, it would possess the Spirit of the living God, moving disciples of Jesus to spread the good news of salvation to the world's dark places and its lost inhabitants.

By coming to Caesarea Philippi, Jesus showed Peter and his disciples that no place or person is God-forsaken, and that God's love is more expansive than they could ever imagine.

The Keys of the Kingdom Given to Peter

Throughout the history of Christian art, beginning in the eighth century, Peter is depicted holding one or two large keys. The keys of Peter are symbols of the authority Jesus bestowed on him. Peter was given the means to open the way to God's kingdom through his preaching and his leadership within the church.

Immediately after Jesus gave Simon the name Peter and declared him the strong foundation of his church, Jesus further described the type of leadership Peter would offer:

> I will give you the keys of the kingdom of heaven, and whatever you bind on earth will be bound in heaven, and whatever you loose on earth will be loosed in heaven. (Matthew 16:19)

The "keys of the kingdom" given to Peter resemble another "key" image from Isaiah the prophet. A certain Eliakim is made "master of the household" and given "the key of the house of David," with the authority to open and shut the gates for those seeking entry into the realm (Isaiah 22:22). Clearly the text of Matthew's Gospel was influenced by this text from the prophet. As keeper of the keys, Peter was made the master of Jesus' household, with the privilege of welcoming people into the church.

The master of the royal household in Israelite culture was the highest official in the land, the one the king appointed to be his prime minister. In ancient Egypt this position was called the vizier, the highest official of the state whom the king appointed to fulfill his sovereign wishes. In other cultures the position was called the king's vicar or chamberlain.

Eliakim was appointed as master of King Hezekiah's household, clothed with the marks of his royal office, and given the authority reserved to the king.

> On that day I will call my servant Eliakim son of Hilkiah, and will clothe him with your robe and bind your sash on him. I will commit your authority to his hand, and he shall be a father to the inhabitants of Jerusalem and to the house of Judah. I will place on his shoulder the key of the house of David; he shall open, and no one shall shut; he shall shut, and no one shall open. (Isaiah 22:21–22)

God says that Eliakim will be a "father" to the inhabitants of the kingdom, exercising familial care to all the citizens of the realm. "The house of David" was the inherited kingship which began with King David and extended in succession to Israel's Messiah, the anticipated "son of David." Holding the key to this house symbolized the authority the king entrusts to his prime minister. The king never relinquishes his authority, but he delegates his authority to his highest official to administer the affairs of the kingdom.

Associated with the power of the key, given to the king's vicar, is the authority to "open" and to "shut": "he shall open, and no one shall shut; he shall shut, and no one shall open." Clearly this refers to much more than the ability to open a door or a gate. It is associated with the authority Jesus gives to Peter, to "bind" and to "loose." The keeper of the keys has authority within the kingdom as administrator and teacher. The language of binding and loosing is terminology used by the rabbis of Jesus' day for authoritative teaching, the creation of *halakah*. This form of teaching refers to the creation of laws and norms based on the authority to interpret the Torah and apply it to particular cases. It is legislation not written down in the Jewish Scriptures but based on the oral interpretation of them, declaring what is permitted and what is not permitted. The rabbis were said to bind when they forbade something and to loose when they permitted it.

This was the position Jesus created for Peter. While still retaining his sovereignty, Jesus entrusted the keys of the kingdom to Peter, his earthly vicar. So Peter was not like a doorkeeper, opening and closing the gates of heaven and deciding who gets in or is left out, as he is sometimes depicted in cartoons or jokes. Rather, the authority of Peter was the regulation of the affairs of the kingdom. He was the vicar of Christ, chamberlain of Christ's household, the prime minister of the realm. Peter was charged with making decisions, based on the teachings of Jesus, which would be authoritative throughout the kingdom:

"Whatever you bind on earth will be bound in heaven, and whatever you loose on earth will be loosed in heaven."

The key of David's house, the authority of the master of the household, was passed down through successive generations during the monarchy of Judah. The title of master of the household is given to Ahishar during the reign of King Solomon (1 Kings 4:6). Other holders of this office specifically mentioned in the Old Testament are Arza under the reign of King Elah (1 Kings 16:9) and Obadiah under the reign of King Ahab (1 Kings 18:3). So it seems that this office and its authority were handed down through the history of Judah's monarchy. Whereas the kingship was an inherited office, passed from father to son, the office of the king's vicar was given by appointment.

Jesus, the eternal Son of David, reigns over an everlasting kingdom and his reign never ends. It seems, though, that the office to which Jesus appointed Peter, his earthly vicar, should continue in every generation. Jesus needs a master of the household for his church, and that need will not diminish until he comes again to reign in glory. We will see later that this is exactly how the early theologians of the church interpreted this passage and the tradition of Peter.

The visions of the book of Revelation announce that Jesus Christ himself holds "the keys of Death and of Hades" and the "key of David." He is the one "who opens and no one will shut, who shuts and no one opens" (Revelation 1:18; 3:7). This power of the keys belongs to Christ alone. He is the Lord who has conquered the underworld and ultimately controls its power. He is the Son of David who holds the key to God's kingdom. As the Lord of light and life, he preserves his church, and the gates of Hades will not prevail against it.

However, the Risen Lord delegates this authority to Peter on earth. The keys are entrusted to Peter and to the church's Petrine office. Peter is the rock on which the church is built; he holds the keys that belong to Christ and is ready to relinquish those keys when Jesus Christ returns in glory at the end of time.

Later in Matthew's Gospel, Jesus extends the power "to bind and to loose" to the church as a whole (Matthew 18:18). The community gathered in his name is invested with his saving presence and power. Its authority to bind and loose, as mentioned in this instance, seems to be mainly juridical, having the authority to declare what is permitted and not permitted, to exclude a person from the community for a persistent offense, and to reconcile that person with the community. This authority of the church, as it was interpreted in the early tradition, includes the authority to interpret and apply the teachings of Jesus, to pronounce doctrinal judgments, and to make disciplinary decisions for the community.

Jesus named only Peter as the rock of his church and gave the keys of the kingdom to him alone. Yet the power of the keys—the authority to bind and loose—is shared in the church when it is joined with Peter. Working through Peter, Jesus preserved in his church the unity of faith that he desired for his followers in the world. As the authoritative leader in the community of the early church, Peter received revelations and made decisions about the church's life and practices that had far-reaching consequences. He was a visible sign and an effective instrument for Christ's church, keeping it solidly built on a firm foundation and protected from all the powers that threaten and could prevail against it.

The Rock Becomes a Stumbling Block

After Peter proclaimed Jesus to be the Messiah, the Son of the living God, and Jesus established Peter as the rock of the church, Jesus began to explain more deeply to his disciples the meaning of his own life. He turned from teaching and healing, which characterized the first half of the Gospel accounts, to preparing his disciples for his cross and death.

Jesus explained that it was not his mission to be a powerful, conquering Messiah or a glorious, regal Son of God. There was no other way, he said, than the way of the cross. Suffering and death would be the inevitable results of his life of self-giving, generous love. This kind of talk was altogether too much for the impulsive Peter. How could the long-awaited king, the great hope of Israel, come to such a disgraceful end? He took Jesus aside and "began to rebuke him, saying, 'God forbid it, Lord! This must never happen to you'" (Matthew 16:22). This showed how far Peter was from understanding the implications of Jesus' mission. Peter thought he knew better than Jesus what it would mean for Jesus to be the Messiah and Son of God. His retort was no doubt motivated by love for Jesus and probably by some fear for his own life. If Jesus was going to be put to death, what might that mean for those who follow him?

Jesus' response to Peter records some of the harshest words recorded from Jesus' mouth. Jesus called Peter "Satan," a tempter.

> [Jesus] turned and said to Peter, "Get behind me, Satan! You are a stumbling block to me; for you are setting your mind not on divine things but on human things." (Matthew 16:23)

Peter was trying to deflect Jesus from the path that God had set before him. Peter was tempting Jesus to take the easy way out, to give in to selfish desires for security and glory. Jesus replied, calling Peter an obstacle, "a stumbling block" in his path. The rock of the church had become an obstruction to Jesus' mission.

Yet Jesus did not say to Peter, "Away with you, Satan," as he had told the devil when he was tempted in the wilderness of Judea. Rather, Jesus told Peter, "Get behind me, Satan," commanding him to resume his position as a follower, walking behind Jesus as he gradually discovered through his mistakes and failures what it meant to be a disciple of his Lord.

Despite the spotlight that shines on the figure of Peter throughout the Gospels, the evangelists refuse to idealize him. They highlight his weaknesses and his breakdowns as well as his sturdy faith and preeminent role among the disciples. Before Peter could truly follow Jesus, he had to learn the cost of discipleship.

> Then Jesus told his disciples, "If any want to become my followers, let them deny themselves and take up their cross and follow me. For those who want to save their life will lose it, and those who lose their life for my sake will find it." (Matthew 16:24–25)

Peter had to learn from Jesus how to replace his self-centered ambition with a willingness to sacrifice himself. He had to learn how to lose himself in Christ, to take up the Messiah's mission, his way of life, and his very identity as his own. Peter had to learn that being a disciple of Jesus means taking up the cross—not grudgingly enduring it but embracing it, willing to suffer for the gospel—and getting behind Jesus to follow his lead.

Surely the Gospel writers intended the lessons of Peter to be lessons necessary for the whole church. Like Peter, the community of disciples must learn that it is not enough to confess Jesus as Messiah and Son of God. We must acknowledge him as the suffering and crucified Lord, and we must express this confession not only in verbal doctrine but also in practice. The church of Jesus Christ must be a cruciform church, shaped and transformed by the cross.

Questions for Reflection and Group Discussion

1. What are some of the reasons Jesus brought Peter and the disciples to the far northern city of Caesarea Philippi?

2. In what ways was Peter's response to Jesus' question, "Who do you say I am?" accurate but inadequate?

3. How does a fuller understanding of Isaiah's prophecy help you to understand Peter's position as keeper of the "keys of the kingdom"?

4. Why do the Gospel writers highlight Peter's weaknesses and his breakdowns along with his sturdy faith and preeminent role among the disciples?

5. What does Peter's transformation from rock to stumbling block teach you about the way of discipleship? What does it teach the church?

5

Peter Follows Jesus
to Jerusalem

The landscape of the Bible is marked periodically with high mountains and hills. In many ancient traditions, these high places were seen as sacred spaces, as meeting points between the earth and heaven, the connection between the physical and spiritual worlds. The divine presence dwelt on the mountaintops, disclosing celestial majesty through storms and lightning, clouds and fire. Israel's psalmist sings: "I lift up my eyes to the hills—from where will my help come? My help comes from the Lord, who made heaven and earth" (Psalm 121:1–2).

As places of prominence throughout the biblical tradition, mountains are locations for theophanies, God's manifestations to human beings. We recall Mount Sinai, where the divine presence was manifested to Moses the lawgiver and Elijah the prophet. Moses went up the mountain to encounter the covenant-making God of Israel. Elijah went to that same mountain and heard God's whispering yet transforming voice.

Two other important mountains in Israel's history are Mount Tabor and Mount Hermon. The psalmist sings to God: "Tabor and Hermon joyously praise your name" (Psalm 89:12). As we remember, Mount Hermon is the high mountain just to the north of Caesarea Philippi. Standing at over 9,000 feet, it remains covered with snow throughout most of the year. Mount Tabor is a much smaller mountain to the southwest of the Sea of Galilee, standing at 1,600 feet. It rises as a single, round hill from the Jezreel Valley. But because of its strategic location, it served as an important fortress throughout much of Israel's history. It flattens off at its top, and from there the whole of central Galilee can be viewed below.

These two mountains, Hermon and Tabor, have vied with each other for the honor of being named the Mount of Transfiguration. The Gospel writers tell us only that Jesus brought Peter, James, and John "up a high mountain" and was transfigured before them. While Mount Hermon would serve as a more dramatic setting for this divine manifestation, Mount Tabor has been chosen by most Christian traditions as the most probable site of Jesus' transfiguration.

Peter's Experience of Jesus Transfigured

On the high mountain, Jesus offers Peter, James, and John a fleeting glimpse and an encouraging insight into the divine mystery veiled by his humanity. The synoptic Gospels express the mysterious nature of this epiphany. Matthew says that the face of Jesus "shone like the sun" (Matthew 17:2). Mark says his clothing became "dazzling white" (Mark 9:3). Luke notes that "Peter and his companions were weighed down with sleep; but since they had stayed awake, they saw his glory" (Luke 9:33).

In Matthew's Gospel, Jesus refers to the disciples' experience on the mountain as a "vision" (Matthew 17:9). This does not reduce the event to an interior or psychological experience—the three disciples are independent witnesses. Rather, describing the encounter as a vision marks this event as a God-given experience, a visualization beyond the ordinary functioning of human eyes. God grants these three chosen disciples the ability to see what otherwise would have been imperceptible to mortal beings. They are caught up in a holy and fascinating vision that they cannot adequately articulate, a mystery that must be contemplated rather than described.

The figures of Moses and Elijah, representing the Torah and the prophets, embody the whole of God's ancient history with Israel. These two central characters of the Old Testament prepare the way for Jesus in the long drama of the world's salvation. Here, the divine drama focuses on the life of Jesus as he begins his journey to Jerusalem, the way that leads to the cross. The Transfiguration, which occurs in the Gospels at the beginning of that way to the cross, serves as a revelation to Peter, James, and John of the fullest meaning of that saving journey.

Peter, filled with awe and reverence at the sight, exclaims how good it is to be in this place and suggests to Jesus that the disciples make "three dwellings, one for you, one for Moses, and one for Elijah" (Mark 9:5). The Greek word here translated as "dwelling" may also mean "tent" or "booth." The word evokes the tent in the wilderness of the exodus in which Moses spoke with God. It also calls to mind the temporary, makeshift shelters erected during the Jewish Feast of Sukkoth (Feast of Booths) to remember Israel's forty-year journey through the desert. Peter's remembrance of the saving path of exodus is a reminder that the disciples are on a similar journey of liberation with Jesus.

The cloud is another familiar image from the exodus journey. From Mount Sinai throughout the journey in the wilderness, the cloud remained with the people as an expression of God's presence overshadowing them along the way. Here on the Mount of Transfiguration, God speaks from the cloud, and after confirming that Jesus is his Son, God says, "listen to him!" (Matthew 17:5). *Listening* means more than hearing words; it signifies a deep and attentive hearing that would allow the words of Jesus to become effective in their lives. As Peter, James, and John continue the journey with Jesus to Jerusalem, they must keep listening to what Jesus is teaching them and living by those teachings.

Listening to Jesus is the way to follow in his footsteps—listening to the word of God that transfigures sinners into forgiven and redeemed people, that transfigures sick and disabled bodies into healed and whole beings, that transfigures bread and wine into his body and blood, and that transfigures suffering and death into resurrected life.

Although it would have been easier to stay on the mountain, Jesus touches his disciples and urges them to get up without fear and walk down the mountain by his side.

> But Jesus came and touched them, saying, "Get up and do not be afraid." And when they looked up, they saw no one except Jesus himself alone. (Matthew 17:7–8)

Peter, who was unable to conceive of Jesus' suffering and being put to death, is enlightened and uplifted through this vision of Jesus' transfigured glory. Yet Peter has to learn that the moment of glory was not given to him for its own sake; it is to help him seek the presence and the will of God in all things. The vision on the mountain will help him realize that his own walking the way of the cross can be filled with radiance. Peter teaches all future disciples that there is only one option for a disciple: we must feel the touch of Jesus, look up from our doubts and fears, and stand up to move forward with Jesus.

Ascending the Mountain and Seeking Transformation

Reaching the top of Mount Tabor today is an exercise in trust. Because the mountain road is too treacherous for tour buses, pilgrims on a group tour must ascend by special taxi vans that drive quickly up and down the mountain throughout the day. A narrow road spirals up the north side of the mountain, providing a dizzying ride with plenty of views for those who dare to keep their eyes open.

In the fourth century, 4,340 rocky steps were built for the Christian pilgrims going to the top of Mount Tabor. The top offers a panorama of much of upper and lower Galilee as well as the other mountains: Mount Gilboa, the mountains of Samaria, Mount Carmel, and on a very clear day, Mount Hermon. Today the mountaintop is a popular spot for hang gliders. Some of the most magnificent cloud formations and sunsets I've seen in the Holy Land have been from this mountain.

The reward at the top is the Church of the Transfiguration. Built in 1924 over the ruins of previous churches dating back to the fourth century, the Franciscan church dominates the top of the mountain. The Italian architect, Antonio Barluzzi, who designed many other churches in the Holy Land, always expresses elements of the biblical text in his architectural design. Approaching the church, the roofline of the façade looks like three tents, paying tribute to Peter's desire to build three tents for Jesus, Moses, and Elijah.

Entering the church, there are two chapels on each side of the entryway, directly beneath the two bell towers. The one on the left is dedicated to Moses and contains an image of him receiving the tablets of stone on Mount Sinai; the chapel on the right is dedicated to Elijah and holds an image of the prophet offering sacrifices on Mount Carmel. The central apse of the church features a glorious mosaic of the Transfiguration that fills the entire church with golden light. On August 6, the Feast of the Transfiguration, the sun strikes a glass plate set into the floor to illuminate the mosaic.

Stairs lead to the lower level of the church where there is a sanctuary covered by a vaulted ceiling. Below the altar are remains from the church of the Byzantine period. The central window behind the altar features peacocks, an ancient Christian symbol for the glorified Christ.

This chapel is an intimate space where I have often celebrated the Eucharist with groups of pilgrims.

When I visit these pilgrimage places, it is my prayer that the *external* physical site will lead to an *interior* spiritual transformation. In Eastern Orthodox spirituality, the Transfiguration expresses the belief that God wants to transform us all into the divine likeness. In the transfiguration of Jesus, we experience a person totally possessed by God, completely on fire with God, perfectly reflecting the divine image. This divinization is what our transforming God would do if we truly gave God free rein in our lives.

We have all had glimpses of this experience: when we touch God in deep prayer, when our hearts are lifted listening to glorious music, when awesome worship fills our spirits with holiness. Yet these glimpses are momentary; in this life we cannot sustain them. The transfiguration of Jesus and our own glimpses of glory remind us that transforming experiences of God's presence are never given to us simply to be enjoyed for their own sake. The gift is given within the context of our vocation to discipleship, to strengthen us for God's calling—a calling that, for the Christian, always includes the call to take up the cross.

Leaving the Church of the Transfiguration grounds to go back down the mountain, there is a small chapel called Descentibus, "for the descent," commemorating the final scene in the Gospel passage:

> As they were coming down the mountain, Jesus ordered them, "Tell no one about the vision until after the Son of Man has been raised from the dead." (Matthew 17:9)

As Moses and Elijah had prepared the way for Jesus, so Jesus prepares the way for Peter, James, and John to travel with him to Jerusalem—the journey that would lead to the cross. Along that way, Jesus will have much to teach his disciples about what it means to call

Jesus the Messiah and Son of God. But they will not truly understand its meaning until he has been raised from the dead.

Each of these biblical mountains—Tabor, Hermon, Sinai, Carmel, and the one to which Jesus was leading his disciples, Mount Zion, the city of Jerusalem—have lessons to teach us. First, ascending the mountain is the culmination of a journey. The journey is a purifying experience, removing us from all that is settled, predictable, and secure. Then we are ready to listen, prepared for the insight and revelation offered on the mountain. Second, the one who ascends the mountain is changed. After we have an experience of encountering God, life is never completely the same again. The path of our life will be different because now we are able to look at life in a new way. And third, upon descending the mountain, there is a task waiting to be taken up. Listening to God's word and gaining insight into God's will gives us a new or fuller mission, a new commitment to our calling to discipleship.

Jesus Teaches Peter about Trust

Following the transfiguration of Jesus on the mountain, Matthew's Gospel contains an extended section in which Jesus offers instructions to the disciples who represent his future church. Speaking to Peter and the other leading disciples, Jesus addresses issues of servant leadership and pastoral care within the community.

In addition to speaking in parables, Jesus also teaches with hyperbole—a figure of speech used to make a point through the use of exaggeration. It is intended to evoke strong feelings or to create a strong impression but is not meant to be taken literally. An example of this form of teaching is found in Jesus' statement about the power of faith.

> For truly I tell you, if you have faith the size of a mustard seed, you will say to this mountain, "Move from here to there," and it will move; and nothing will be impossible for you. (Matthew 17:20)

Jesus chided his disciples for their "little faith" when they panicked during a storm on the Sea of Galilee (Matthew 8:26), when Peter began to sink while walking on the water (14:31), when they worried about not having bread for their next meal (16:8), and when they were unable to rebuke a demon from a young boy (17:20). In all of these cases, the disciples had taken their eyes off Jesus and looked only at the obstacles. And so their faith faltered when put to the test.

In using the images of the mustard seed and the mountain, Jesus again appeals to objects familiar to the disciples. The mustard seed, the smallest of all seeds, may have been the smallest thing Galileans ever experienced. In contrast, a mountain was probably the largest thing they ever considered. Through his hyperbolic teaching, Jesus tells his disciples that just a small amount of faith, when placed confidently in him, can accomplish great things, even what seems impossible.

Contemplating this teaching of Jesus, in the context of the mission he has entrusted to Peter and the other disciples, can instill within us deeper reliance on Jesus and greater confidence in the mission he has given to his church. Faith is our realization that what is impossible for us is possible for God. Faith leads us into the realm of the impossible—like trusting in the midst of storms, walking on water, providing bread for the hungry, and casting out the powers of evil. Peter can be our example as we see him grow in faith and learn to keep his eyes on Jesus.

Following this teaching on faith, Matthew's Gospel recounts a curious incident in Capernaum. The tax collectors of the temple tax ask Peter, "Does your teacher not pay the temple tax?" (Matthew 17:24). Every Jewish man was charged an annual tax, assessed by the religious authorities, for the support of the temple. Matthew's Greek text says that the tax was two drachmas, an amount equivalent to the half shekel in Jewish coinage. Peter replies that, yes, Jesus pays the tax.

But when Peter goes "home," presumably his own house, Jesus asks him, "What do you think, Simon? From whom do kings of the earth take toll or tribute? From their children or from others?" These tolls and tributes refer to custom taxes and census taxes, the types of taxes generally collected by Roman authorities. Peter answers correctly, "From others," knowing that kings don't collect taxes from their own children but from those who are not members of the royal family. Jesus' point was that Jesus and his disciples are living in God's kingdom as his sons and daughters. However, because they live in the world and must be subject to earthly authorities, Jesus indicates that he and Peter ought to pay the tax. Then Jesus suggests this peculiar way that Peter should make the payment.

> So that we do not give offense to them, go to the sea and cast a hook; take the first fish that comes up; and when you open its mouth, you will find a coin; take that and give it to them for you and me. (Matthew 17:27)

Jesus' main teaching here seems to be twofold. First, children of God's kingdom can rely on their Father for all provisions, even for taxes he would not impose on them. Second, disciples should pay earthly taxes so as not to give "offense," a word here that suggests creating scandal or being a stumbling block to others.

Many commentators explain this odd episode as folklore. Yet Jesus teaches with a story many fishermen would relate to. Fish in the Sea of Galilee have a habit of picking up things in their mouths from the bottom of the lake. St. Peter's fish, the *Tilapia galilaea,* often pick up small pebbles in their mouths, and fishermen tell stories of finding bottle caps as well in the mouths of these fish.

The temple taxes were collected during the week before Passover, when the seawater is growing warmer and spawning begins. About this time, the tilapia can be found moving gravel to build spawning pits. These tilapia are known to carry their young in their wide mouths until they are large enough to protect themselves and leave. So finding a coin in the mouth of these fish might not be as outlandish as it sounds.

The fact that this single coin paid the taxes for both Jesus and Peter may be another indicator that they both shared the same house in Capernaum. Every Jewish male aged twenty and over was required to pay the tax; this story suggests that Jesus and Peter were the two adult men living in the house of Peter.

The coin that Jesus tells Peter he will find is called in Greek the *stater*, worth about four drachma or about one shekel in Jewish coinage. Whenever I go to one of the restaurants around the Sea of Galilee to eat St. Peter's fish, I always ask if they have caught any with a shekel in its mouth. Invariably they will bring me a fried fish, its comblike dorsal fin extending to the edge of the plate, its eyes looking up at me, and a shekel stuffed into its open mouth.

Jesus Teaches Peter about Mercy in the Church

As Jesus continues to teach Peter and those who will have leadership responsibilities in his church, he consistently insists that they care for the weak and the lost. His teaching is prompted by a question from his disciples, "Who is the greatest in the kingdom of heaven?" (Matthew 18:1). Jesus dramatically illustrates his response by placing a child in the midst of them. The greatest in God's kingdom, he says, are those who become like children, shedding status and pretensions, living in a spirit of humility. Jesus then adds that disciples must not only become like children, but they must also welcome and serve those who are powerless like children. This is the way to true leadership within his church.

As Jesus continues his teaching, he warns the leaders of his church not to place obstacles in the way of the "little ones," those who are the most weak and vulnerable members of the community.

> If any of you put a stumbling block before one of these little ones who believe in me, it would be better for you if a great millstone were fastened around your neck and you were drowned in the depth of the sea. (Matthew 18:6)

A "stumbling block" represents some sinful or scandalous attitude or behavior that harms the faith of these little ones. Jesus uses a strong image to convey the serious consequences of causing those who are weak in faith to sin or lose hope. A millstone is a large grinding stone turned by a donkey. A millstone around a person's neck would ensure a rapid descent to the bottom of the sea. Jesus admits that "occasions for stumbling are bound to come" in his church run by fragile people in a sin-soaked world. But this inevitability of scandal does not excuse it: "[W]oe to the one by whom the stumbling block comes!" If Jesus' church is to reach out to those who are lost and most vulnerable, then it cannot tolerate pastoral leaders who take advantage of their position and bring harm to them.

Through the parable of the lost sheep, Jesus emphasizes the extraordinary lengths a pastor should go in recovering one who has gone astray.

> If a shepherd has a hundred sheep, and one of them has gone astray, does he not leave the ninety-nine on the mountains and go in search of the one that went astray? And if he finds it, truly I tell you, he rejoices over it more than over the ninety-nine that never went astray. So it is not the will of your Father in heaven that one of these little ones should be lost. (Matthew 18:12–14)

Those who shepherd the church must always seek out the weak and errant members. Likewise, pastors should rejoice greatly over the recovery of one missing member because the Father in heaven does not wish any of the little ones to be lost.

Jesus continues to lay the foundation for a merciful church by offering a three-step procedure for confronting a fellow disciple who sins within the community (Matthew 18:15–17). The first step is a private conversation directly with the offender. This attempt to persuade the wrongdoer averts bitter gossip and seeks reconciliation. If no progress is made, then two or three witnesses should be introduced into the process. If this small group of peers fails to produce reconciliation, then the case should be brought before the whole local church. The purpose of the procedure is always to restore the offender to the community. If all these attempts fail, then the wrongdoer must be treated like "a Gentile and a tax collector." In the Jewish arena, these groups represent an outsider and a sinner. However, considering Jesus' unrelenting compassion for Gentiles and tax collectors, perhaps he is saying that his church should never give up on anyone. Even if the church must exclude a wayward member, the goal must always be to seek repentance from the wrongdoer. The pastoral concern of the community for an errant member never completely ends.

Peter poses the final question of this section of Jesus' teaching. He wants to know the extent of mercy that he should practice within the church.

> Then Peter came and said to him, "Lord, if another member of the church sins against me, how often should I forgive? As many as seven times?" Jesus said to him, "Not seven times, but, I tell you, seventy-seven times." (Matthew 18:21–22)

Perhaps Peter is concerned to clarify the three-step process Jesus has just described for reconciling errant members of the church. He poses a hypothetical case about a fellow disciple who wrongs him over and over. He wants to know where he can draw the line and stop forgiving. Will it be enough to forgive the same offense seven times? Peter assumes he is being generous by suggesting seven times as a reasonable limit. Surely after the third or fourth wrong we may assume that the offender is not going to change and doesn't deserve more forgiveness. Jesus' answer, however, indicates that forgiveness must be unending.

The response of Jesus, "Not seven times, but, I tell you, seventy-seven times," alludes to the Old Testament character Lamech, a descendant of Cain. Lamech boasted that he would exact overwhelming vengeance on anyone who dared to attack him: "If Cain is avenged sevenfold, truly Lamech seventy-sevenfold" (Genesis 4:24). With this ancient allusion, Jesus presents forgiveness as the polar opposite of revenge. Disciples must renounce the instinct to retaliate against someone who repeatedly wrongs them and to forgive them instead.

To drive home his teaching to Peter and all those listening, Jesus tells another parable about a king and the quality of mercy within his kingdom.

For this reason the kingdom of heaven may be compared to a king who wished to settle accounts with his slaves. When he began the reckoning, one who owed him ten thousand talents was brought to him; and, as he could not pay, his lord ordered him to be sold, together with his wife and children and all his possessions, and payment to be made. So the slave fell on his knees before him, saying, "Have patience with me, and I will pay you everything." And out of pity for him, the lord of that slave released him and forgave him the debt. But that same slave, as he went out, came upon one of his fellow slaves who owed him a hundred denarii; and seizing him by the throat, he said, "Pay what you owe." Then his fellow slave fell down and pleaded with him, "Have patience with me, and I will pay you." But he refused; then he went and threw him into prison until he would pay the debt. When his fellow slaves saw what had happened, they were greatly distressed, and they went and reported to their lord all that had taken place. Then his lord summoned him and said to him, "You wicked slave! I forgave you all that debt because you pleaded with me. Should you not have had mercy on your fellow slave, as I had mercy on you?" And in anger his lord handed him over to be tortured until he would pay his entire debt. So my heavenly Father will also do to every one of you, if you do not forgive your brother or sister from your heart. (Matthew 18:23–35)

What a master storyteller Jesus was. The power of the parable is found in the varied contrasts. First, we see the huge debt owed by the slave—a massive amount that could never be repaid—compared with the rather small debt owed to the slave. Next, we see the king's heartfelt and merciful decision to forgive the slave's debt contrasted with the slave's brutal and merciless response to his fellow slave. Because the slave had already been forgiven an astounding and unpayable obligation by his king, he should have lived his life in light of that amazing grace.

This parable shows us that we must be constant in our forgiving because God's forgiving mercy toward us knows no bounds. Each of us is like that slave. We are sinners who owe the Lord a staggering amount, but whose debt has been pardoned by the merciful King. Since God has forgiven us such a debt, how much more willing should we be to forgive others? Peter's question addressed a human problem from a human perspective. This parable of the kingdom grounds forgiveness in the very nature of God.

Jesus urges disciples to "forgive your brother or sister from your heart." Although we have been lovingly forgiven by our God, we can open our lives to receive that forgiveness only when we forgive others from our hearts. As we forgive one another, we allow that tremendous forgiveness of God to take hold of our lives and renew us from within. God's forgiveness then overflows from our lives into Christ's church.

Throughout Matthew's presentation of Jesus' teachings on church leadership, Jesus has spoken about the church community with utmost mercy and tenderness. He has referred to members of the church with such terms as humble children, little ones, lost sheep, and brothers and sisters. Although confrontation and discipline are often necessary within the community, the goal is always reconciliation and returning the strays to the fold. Assuring the church of his ongoing presence, Jesus demonstrates that its sacred work must always be permeated with humility, familial love, and a passion for forgiveness.

The Challenges and Rewards of Discipleship

As Jesus continues to approach Jerusalem with his disciples, he keeps teaching them about the cost of discipleship. Living under the reign of God affects everything in a person's life, from major decisions to style of living. Jesus' teachings, responding to the questions of his disciples, remind me of the words of Micah 6:6–8. God's people ask several questions about what God requires of them. The prophet then responds by stating God's three requirements for what is "good" for his people: "to do justice, and to love kindness, and to walk humbly with your God."

As Jesus teaches his disciples about the requirements for entering into the life of God's kingdom, he warns them about the dangers of riches. Again Jesus teaches with an amazing hyperbole that Peter will not soon forget.

> Then Jesus said to his disciples, "Truly I tell you, it will be hard for a rich person to enter the kingdom of heaven. Again I tell you, it is easier for a camel to go through the eye of a needle than for someone who is rich to enter the kingdom of God." When the disciples heard this, they were greatly astounded and said, "Then who can be saved?" But Jesus looked at them and said, "For mortals it is impossible, but for God all things are possible." (Matthew 19:23–26)

The camel was the largest animal in Palestine, and the eye of a needle used for sewing was one of the smallest openings anyone at the time could imagine. Jesus is telling his disciples that the attraction to wealth and possessions is so alluring that a rich person, with his or her own might, is unable to resist. Just as it is impossible for a camel to crawl through a needle's eye, it is humanly impossible to share in God's kingdom while depending on riches, privilege, and security.

Israel's prophets had taught how yearning for wealth can lead to the exploitation of the poor, neglect of one's covenant obligations, and a divided heart. The words of Jesus are set within this prophetic challenge to the corrosive power of wealth. Yet, when the disciples hear this maxim of Jesus, they are "greatly astounded." They apparently assume that wealth is a sign of God's favor. So, if those who enjoy God's favor find it so difficult to enter God's kingdom, then how can anyone do so?

The heart of Jesus' teaching, for Peter and all the disciples, lies in Jesus' response to the question, "Then who can be saved?" His answer implies that it is impossible from a human standpoint to overcome the powerful lure of wealth and to be dependent on God alone. The process of being saved, the transformation that takes place as a person enters the life that Jesus offers, is impossible for human beings to achieve on their own, "but for God all things are possible." Just as God gave us mortal life as a gift, God can save us from sin and death and give us eternal life.

Salvation cannot be earned by anyone. No amount of good work, sacrifice, and self-denial can ever merit salvation for anyone. Salvation is given to us out of the merciful love of God. By doing God's will and following in the way of Jesus, we rid ourselves of all the obstacles that stand in the way of God's saving initiative. By joining our own sacrificial deeds and self-giving actions to the sacrifice of Jesus Christ, we cooperate with God's salvation and open our lives to the grace God offers us through faith.

Peter's follow-up question to Jesus is natural enough, but it seems inappropriate at this point. Peter's personality is impulsive, straightforward, and often blunt. So he asks the sixty-four-thousand-dollar question that everyone wants to ask but is too timid to do so.

> Then Peter said in reply, "Look, we have left everything and followed you. What then will we have?" (Matthew 19:27)

In effect, Peter is asking, "After giving up so much for you, what are we going to get out of it?" If it is impossible for human beings to save themselves, have we given up everything for nothing? Would we be just as well off if we were still fishing? Are our human efforts pointless?

Jesus could have scolded Peter and told him that he had missed the point of discipleship once again. Yet Jesus uses Peter's demanding inquiry to teach him. The purpose of following Jesus is not to earn a reward but to open oneself to the fullness of life that God offers.

> Jesus said to them, "Truly I tell you, at the renewal of all things, when the Son of Man is seated on the throne of his glory, you who have followed me will also sit on twelve thrones, judging the twelve tribes of Israel. And everyone who has left houses or brothers or sisters or father or mother or children or fields, for my name's sake, will receive a hundredfold, and will inherit eternal life. But many who are first will be last, and the last will be first." (Matthew 19:28–30)

Jesus assures Peter that their commitment to Jesus is not in vain and that the Twelve will have glorious roles in the age to come. As Jewish literature foresees, the twelve tribes of Israel will be regathered and renewed in the age of the Messiah. Jesus tells the Twelve that they will rule over this renewed people of God that Jesus is establishing. Even though now they seem to have given up everything, their losses will be made up many times over, and they will experience the fullness of life forever. Even though now they seem poor and persecuted, counted "last" in the eyes of the world, they will be "first" as they share in God's glory.

Peter took all these words of Jesus to heart; we will see this as we follow Peter's footsteps to Jerusalem and then eventually to Rome. We will witness how he actualized these words of Jesus in his ministry of church leadership and pastoral care throughout his life of service.

Questions for Reflection and Group Discussion

1. What new insights have you received into the meaning of Jesus' transfiguration on the mountain?

2. God tells the disciples to "listen" to Jesus as he teaches them the way of discipleship on the journey toward Jerusalem. In what ways do these words challenge you? What keeps you engaged and motivated along the path of discipleship?

3. What are some of the ways that Jesus teaches Peter about maintaining a merciful church?

4. What are the lessons for you in Jesus' parable of the merciful king and the unmerciful servant?

5. What is the point, for Peter and for the church, of Jesus' saying about the camel and the needle? How do you grapple with Jesus' warnings about the dangers of riches?

6

Peter Enters Jesus' Passion in Jerusalem

There are basically two directions to guide pilgrims through the Holy Land. One way is to start by exploring Jerusalem and its surroundings and then travel to Galilee and the sites around the Sea of Galilee. But when I lead pilgrimage groups, I always begin in Galilee, in Nazareth and the towns around the lake, and then follow the path of the Gospels "up to Jerusalem."

Whenever the Bible states that people are traveling to Jerusalem, it is always described as an upward journey. Even though the way from Galilee to Jerusalem is southward, which we commonly designate as downward, the biblical language always specifies an approach "up" to Jerusalem. The reason for this is twofold. First, the approach to Jerusalem from every direction is toward a higher elevation. The altitude of the city is about 2,500 feet, and it is surrounded by valleys. Second, because Jerusalem is the holy city, the place of God's temple throughout the biblical period, pilgrims must raise their minds and their hearts as they approach the city because of God's unique dwelling there.

My first experience of the Holy Land did not begin in Galilee but in Jerusalem. I came first in 1978 as a student of theology. I decided to spend the summer months there in order to learn some biblical

Hebrew, study the Jewish tradition, and start exploring the land. I lived and studied at Ratisbonne Monastery, a center for Christians interested in Jewish studies. The program was later named in honor of St. Peter, the Jewish disciple and first leader of Christ's church, and called Institut Saint-Pierre de Sion-Ratisbonne, Centre Chrétien d'Études Juives.

Marie-Alphonse Ratisbonne, together with his brother, founded the Congregation of Our Lady of Sion in mid-nineteenth-century Paris, "to witness in the church and in the world that God continues to be faithful in his love for the Jewish people." Shortly afterward, Father Ratisbonne came to Palestine. There he established the Ecce Homo convent for the Sisters of Zion on the Via Dolorosa in the old city of Jerusalem. The site began as a convent, orphanage, and school, and later developed into a center for Jewish-Christian relations. Then two decades later, he began the construction of Ratisbonne Monastery in the new city of Jerusalem.

In May 1948, the monastery opened its gates to Jewish women and children evacuated from the Gush Etzion settlements when they were under attack by the Arab forces after Israel was declared a state by the United Nations. When I arrived in 1978, there was more hope for the conflict than there is today. The Camp David Accords were being negotiated, which would lead the following year to the peace agreement between Egypt and Israel. Some years later, Ratisbonne Monastery served as the site for negotiations between the Holy See and the State of Israel, leading to an accord and diplomatic relations in 1993.

While I was living in Jerusalem, I came to know the great work of the Congregation of Our Lady of Sion, not only the classes, research, and lectures of the Center for Jewish Studies but also the variety of pastoral ministries in the Holy Land performed by the priests, brothers, and the sisters of Zion. They continue working in the Holy Land and other places throughout the world to improve Christian-Jewish relations and to witness to God's faithful love for the Jewish people. A few years later in 1981, I spent a year in Jerusalem as part of my studies at the Pontifical Biblical Institute. The institute, run by the Jesuit order, is conveniently located between the King David Hotel and the Jaffa Gate of the Old City. In a cooperative program with Hebrew University, I studied biblical Hebrew, biblical archaeology and geography, and the histories of Israel and early Christianity. I've returned several times since then, most recently in March of 2013, thanks to the hospitality of Joseph Doan Cong Nguyen, SJ, and Antony Sinnamuthu, SJ. As previously mentioned, I was privileged to be staying with the Jesuits there on the evening that Pope Francis, the first Jesuit pope, was elected. A year later I led a pilgrimage in Palestine and Israel at the same time Pope Francis made his pilgrimage there.

Every time I go "up to Jerusalem," either on my own or with astounded pilgrims, I recite or chant some of the psalms of ascent (Psalms 120–134)—the fourteen psalms specially designated as psalms to be sung during pilgrimage to Jerusalem. I love Psalm 122, which begins and ends with these words.

> I was glad when they said to me,
> "Let us go to the house of the Lord!"
> Our feet are standing
> within your gates, O Jerusalem. . . .
> Pray for the peace of Jerusalem:
> "May they prosper who love you.
> Peace be within your walls,
> and security within your towers."
> For the sake of my relatives and friends
> I will say, "Peace be within you."
> For the sake of the house of the Lord our God,
> I will seek your good.
> (Psalm 122:1–2, 6–9)

The Entry into Jerusalem

Jesus and Peter must have gone up to Jerusalem many times throughout their lives for the annual pilgrim feasts. But the Gospels of Matthew, Mark, and Luke record only one journey to Jerusalem during Jesus' adult life, and it's the culmination of his ministry. It is a journey to the cross, to the summit of his life's work, when, as John's Gospel says, Jesus will be lifted up in order to draw all people to himself (John 12:32).

Jesus and his disciples at last reach the final steps of their long, resolute journey to Jerusalem. After passing through the Jordan Valley, they turn westward at Jericho to begin the steep ascent to the holy city. Arriving at the summit of the Mount of Olives, they see the city with its temple gleaming in the sunlight. Like so many pilgrims to Jerusalem before and after them, their hearts are lifted at the sight—holy Zion, the city of the great King.

I love to introduce pilgrims to the city from the Mount of Olives. It offers a magnificent view of the entire city. As we look across the Kidron Valley, the eastern walls of the city lead our eyes up to the temple mount. The temple of Israel stood on this site in the days of Jesus until its destruction by the Romans in AD 70. Today it is dominated by the Dome of the Rock, a shrine important to Islam. Behind the temple mount is the Church of the Holy Sepulcher, containing the sites of both Jesus' crucifixion and resurrection.

Although Jesus could have slipped into the city undetected under cover of darkness, he made careful plans for his entrance into the city as a messianic act. Again he offers a visual teaching and an enacted parable of the upside-down values of God's kingdom. The familiar scene of a conquering king parading gloriously into a city is transformed into a scene that embodies the humble dignity that typifies God's reign. This king is dressed not in royal splendor or military trappings but in the simple dress of a Jewish teacher. He is meek and humble, not bellicose and splendorous. He rides not a mighty warhorse but a young donkey. This is a king like no other. The mixed signals perplex the citizens and the many pilgrims in the city.

> A very large crowd spread their cloaks on the road, and others cut branches from the trees and spread them on the road. The crowds that went ahead of him and that followed were shouting, "Hosanna to the Son of David! Blessed is the one who comes in the name of the Lord! Hosanna in the highest heaven!" When he entered Jerusalem, the whole city was in turmoil, asking, "Who is this?" The crowds were saying, "This is the prophet Jesus from Nazareth in Galilee." (Matthew 21:8–11)

The people of Jerusalem are accustomed to crowds of high-spirited pilgrims entering the city for the feasts, but when Jesus makes his entrance, the whole city is in turmoil. People are asking about the identity of the one who enters with such a flourish. The Gospel narrative confronts us, its readers, with the same question: "Who is this?"

The crowds began saying, "This is the prophet Jesus from Nazareth in Galilee." Their answer, like that of Peter earlier in the Gospel, is accurate but inadequate. The question, "Who is this?" hovers over the remainder of the Gospel account of Jesus' last days. Each event of his final days in Jerusalem presents a partial and continually developing answer to this critical question.

Peter at the Last Supper

Jesus' triumphal entry into Jerusalem soon turns to tragedy as the climactic actions of the Gospel begin to unfold. The crowd's jubilant shouts of "Hosanna" will within a few days distort into cries of "crucify him." As in the liturgy of Palm Sunday, the joyful procession is only a prelude for the proclamation of the Passion.

Before the arrival of the feast, Jesus makes plans to celebrate the Passover with his disciples. Luke's Gospel says that Jesus sent Peter and

John to prepare the Passover meal. As Jesus had arranged, a man in the city showed them "a large room upstairs" where they made plans for the ritual supper (Luke 22:12).

The second-story room of houses in Jerusalem were often used for guests, especially for pilgrims who came to celebrate the feasts in the city. The "upper room," described in the Gospels as the place where Jesus celebrated the Last Supper with his disciples, was located on Mount Zion, the western hill of Jerusalem. Sometimes called the *Cenacle* ("supper room"), it is today an empty room with a few indicators of its former use as both a Crusader church and an Islamic mosque.

At the time of Jesus, festive meals such as the Passover supper were eaten while reclining on cushions. The elaborate rituals of the Seder meal are not detailed in the Gospels; neither is the traditional recounting of the story of Exodus. The only parts of the meal highlighted in this account are those to which Jesus introduced a radical new meaning. The food of the Passover—the unleavened bread—is identified as the body of Jesus. The cup of wine is identified as the blood of Jesus, the blood of the covenant poured out as the new covenant. Although the upper room is empty today, the events that took place there live at the heart of the Christian faith, renewed over and over again every day across the world.

John's Gospel presents the Last Supper in a radically different way than the other Gospels do. The evangelist introduces the meal by telling us that Jesus knows that his time to leave the world has come. Then the Gospel summarizes the entire life and death of Jesus as an act of self-giving love: "Having loved his own who were in the world, he loved them to the end" (John 13:1). On the night before his death, Jesus dramatically shows his disciples what his life has been about and what his death will mean. In place of the institution of the Eucharist as recounted in the other three Gospels, John's Gospel narrates how Jesus washes the feet of his disciples. Both Eucharist and foot washing, in different ways, express the self-giving of Jesus. Jesus is the humble servant who gives his life for others as an expression of his faithful love, and he loves his disciples to the very end.

In New Testament times the unpaved roads became extremely dusty in dry weather and awfully muddy when it rained. Sandals gave little protection for the feet of travelers, so the servant of the house was always ready with a towel and washbowl to wash the feet of guests as they arrived. By taking the role of the servant, Jesus shocks his disciples with his humility and gives them a lesson they would not soon forget. In fact, this simple gesture has been memorialized by Christians through the ages as a prophetic demonstration of a disciple's lifestyle.

> And during supper Jesus, knowing that the Father had given all things into his hands, and that he had come from God and was going to God, got up from the table, took off his outer robe, and tied a towel around himself. Then he poured water into a basin and began to wash the disciples' feet and to wipe them with the towel that was tied around him. He came to Simon Peter, who said to him, "Lord, are you going to wash my feet?" Jesus answered, "You do not know now what I am doing, but later you will understand." Peter said to him, "You will never wash my feet." (John 13:3–8)

Peter strongly resists Jesus' actions. Again we see Peter's independence and self-sufficiency rise to the surface. It is difficult for the self-reliant Peter to be served by another. Yet Jesus plainly demonstrates that being a disciple means not only serving others but also learning how to be served by others. Peter has to learn to depend on others, to realize his need to be helped, before he can be a true servant like Jesus.

Jesus' actions reject human relationships characterized by domination. He instead models relationships rooted in self-giving and interdependent ministry. Jesus responds to Peter's resistance by saying, "Unless I wash you, you have no share with me." In other words, unless Peter allows Jesus to wash his feet, Peter cannot be his disciple. The key to Peter's being a disciple and participating in the ministry of Jesus is expressed in this act of foot washing—that is, sharing in the self-giving love that will bring Jesus' life to an end.

The impulsive Peter then urges Jesus to wash even more: "Lord, not my feet only but also my hands and my head!" Jesus' response, "One who has bathed does not need to wash, except for the feet, but is entirely clean," is a reference to the once-only Christian baptism. Foot washing is a partial and limited service that must be constantly repeated. But the cleansing Jesus spoke of happens only once, as followers are baptized ("bathed") into the death and resurrection of Jesus. In the same way, Jesus gave himself only once on the cross, yet his smaller acts of sacrificial love are repeated frequently through his disciples.

> After he had washed their feet, had put on his robe, and had returned to the table, he said to them, "Do you know what I have done to you?" You call me Teacher and Lord—and you are right, for that is what I am. So if I, your Lord and Teacher, have washed your feet, you also ought to wash one another's feet. For I have set you an example, that you also should do as I have done to you. (John 13:12–15)

Do *we* understand what Jesus has done? He calls his symbolic action "an example," a deed that his disciples must imitate for others. Because the action of Jesus is an example, it can be expressed by disciples through deeds of compassion, material help to those in need, forgiveness of offenses, and a host of other actions that display sacrificial love for others. We all are called to love in this way. We are to love "to the end"—to the end of our lives and as completely as we can.

Peter would long remember this moment. The foot washing foreshadows and illumines the self-giving involved in Jesus' death on the cross. The Teacher who washes the feet of his disciples corresponds to the Good Shepherd who lays down his life for his sheep. At the end of John's Gospel, Peter will be commissioned to care for the sheep of the risen Christ. Following the example of Jesus, Peter will shepherd the flock of his Lord, even to the point of laying down his own life for them. But first Peter must make it through this night of testing and enter with Jesus into his passion.

The Rock of Strength Begins to Crumble

Although the Gospels show us many of Peter's strengths and highlight his unique role among the disciples, they also spotlight his tragic weaknesses and failures. The same Peter who professed the truth of Jesus' identity and is called to be the foundation of the church is the same disciple Jesus calls a tempter and a stumbling block. Peter's faith allows him to walk on the turbulent waters, but he is overcome with doubt and fear. Peter, who leaves all to follow Jesus and witnesses his transfigured glory, also underestimates the necessity of forgiveness and seeks a reward for his efforts. We are shown the flaws in Peter's character—the chips in the Rock—but we are also shown, through praise and criticism of Peter throughout the Gospels, how God is working through the life of this great disciple.

One of Peter's chief troubles as a disciple is his inability to accept the suffering of Jesus. Peter refuses to believe the reality of the cross and its implications for his own life. The cross is the stumbling block that causes Peter and many halfhearted followers to fall away. Indeed, as Jesus leaves the upper room with his disciples and travels with them to the Mount of Olives, he predicts that during the night of his betrayal and arrest, all his disciples will run away and leave him alone.

> When they had sung the hymn, they went out to the Mount of Olives. Then Jesus said to them, "You will all become deserters because of me this night; for it is written, 'I will strike the shepherd, and the sheep of the flock will be scattered.' But after I am raised up, I will go ahead of you to Galilee." (Matthew 26:30–32)

The failure of the disciples is described through a citation of the prophet Zechariah. Jesus identifies himself as "the shepherd." When he is struck down, the sheep of his flock will be scattered. Although Jesus has defined discipleship as taking up the cross and following him (Matthew 16:24), when the test comes, all will desert him. Yet Jesus adds to this scene a hint of a hopeful future. He says that these scattered disciples will be gathered together again when he is risen, and once again in Galilee, Jesus will lead them as a shepherd leads his flock. Although they will abandon him that night, in faithful love he will restore them to discipleship.

In this same scene in Luke's Gospel, Jesus issues a challenging yet hopeful exhortation directly to Peter. His words summarize the ordeal of Peter's discipleship during the passion account and anticipate his role beyond those events and into the life of the church.

> "Simon, Simon, listen! Satan has demanded to sift all of you like wheat, but I have prayed for you that your own faith may not fail; and you, when once you have turned back, strengthen your brothers." (Luke 22:31–32)

Jesus speaks of three aspects of Peter's testing: his sifting by Satan, his turning back to follow Jesus, and his role in strengthening his brothers. Satan will severely test the disciples for the purpose of destroying their faith. By this point, the devil has already taken Judas, and now he is attempting to take the other disciples too. Indeed, that very night Peter's fear will overpower his faith as he denies his Lord. Jesus assures Peter that he has prayed for him so that his faith will not collapse in the time of crisis. And though Peter will falter in faith, he will weep bitterly over his failing, which will mark the beginning of his turning back to Jesus.

Jesus trusts that Peter will repent and return to following him. In fact, in the Acts of the Apostles, Luke describes Peter's pivotal role among the other disciples and his ministry of strengthening them.

Peter's complete return to Jesus is not brought about by his own initiative but through the sovereign initiative of his risen Lord. And the strength of Peter's testimony to the resurrection convinces others to join in the affirmation of faith as he gathers the disciples again in Jerusalem and becomes the leading figure in the infant church.

But here, on the Mount of Olives, Peter shows himself at his worst—proud, brash, and arrogant.

> Peter said to him, "Though all become deserters because of you, I will never desert you." Jesus said to him, "Truly I tell you, this very night, before the cock crows, you will deny me three times." Peter said to him, "Even though I must die with you, I will not deny you." (Matthew 26:33–35)

Peter refuses to accept his own dark side and to consider the possibility of his own failure. Although Peter allows that Jesus might be right about the other disciples, he is certain that his own faith will never be shaken. Peter is convinced that his commitment is stronger than that of the others, that his discipleship can overcome all obstacles. This is the arrogant self-confidence of a man bound for failure. Peter's overconfidence in his abilities and his lack of humble reliance on God leave him unprepared for the crisis he will soon face.

Jesus knows Peter's weakness, but he still allows him to fail. Jesus obviously loves Peter, but he does not remove the challenges that face him. The passion of Jesus becomes the point of crisis for Peter. The contrast between the words of Peter and those of Jesus could not be sharper. Peter says to Jesus, "I will never desert you," and increasing his bravado, "I will not deny you." Never? Jesus responds to Peter's presumptuousness by stating that Peter will abandon him that very night and that he will deny him, in fact, three times. As Peter affirms his undying loyalty to Jesus, he sets himself up for failure. When the challenge of Jesus' passion arrives, Peter will demonstrate how fragile his commitment really is.

The irony of this narrative becomes apparent in the scenes that follow: Peter sleeps rather than prays with Jesus; he flees at the arrest of Jesus; and he swears with an oath that he does not know Jesus. Peter's bluster holds a lesson for all future disciples. We may be willing, but we are weak. We may be completely sincere in our commitment to follow Jesus, but because that confidence is rooted in our own ego, we may not have the strength to carry it out. If we do not recognize our vulnerability, then we have set ourselves up for failure. Rather than trust ourselves never to fail, it is better to place our confidence in a power beyond our own, to put our trust in Jesus, who promises to restore us with faithful love when we do fail.

The Prayer of Jesus and the Sleep of Peter

After the Last Supper, Jesus goes with his disciples across the Kidron Valley to a place called Gethsemane, at the foot of the Mount of Olives. He knows that Judas his betrayer will follow and that he will bring soldiers to arrest him. If Jesus were to choose escape, it would be easy enough to do. He could simply continue walking up the Mount of Olives, over its top, and into the Judean desert. But Jesus stops at Gethsemane, where he prays and agonizes over his pending arrest and passion. Only in prayer can Jesus discern whether to stay or retreat.

As Jesus arrives at Gethsemane, he knows full well that Peter's pledge of faithful discipleship and loyalty in crisis will prove to be well-intentioned but empty chatter. Jesus departs from the larger group of disciples in order to pray, taking with him only Peter and the two sons of Zebedee. These are the same three disciples Jesus invited to be with him at the transfiguration. As Jesus had taken Peter, James, and John away to a high mountain to reveal his glory to them alone, now Jesus takes the same inner circle of disciples out of the crowded city to a quiet olive grove. In both scenes, Jesus takes the three disciples aside from the others to reveal the depth of his mission. As they witnessed Jesus in glory, they now see him in weakness and anguish as he faces impending death. If they are to truly know Jesus, they must understand his suffering as well as his glory.

> Then Jesus went with them to a place called Gethsemane; and he said to his disciples, "Sit here while I go over there and pray." He took with him Peter and the two sons of Zebedee, and began to be grieved and agitated. Then he said to them, "I am deeply grieved, even to death; remain here, and stay awake with me." And going a little farther, he threw himself on the ground and prayed, "My Father, if it is possible, let this cup pass from me; yet not what I want but what you want." (Matthew 26:36–39)

This scene demonstrates the fullness of Jesus' humanity. He is grieved, agitated, distressed, fearful, and worried, needing the supportive companionship of his dearest friends as he prepares for the ordeal to come. He urges his closest companions to remain near him and stay awake.

The scene in Gethsemane is the most intimate portrait the Gospels offer of Jesus at prayer. In this quiet place, Jesus "threw himself on the ground" and began to pray in anguish. The prostrate position with his face to the ground is a stance of complete submission and respect. Jesus begs for deliverance—"let this cup pass from me"; but at the same time he prays for a resolute commitment to God's will, a poignant paradox that is typical of honest prayer from the heart in times of crisis. Jesus knows that suffering and death lay ahead of him, yet he also knows that he must go on. The cup of suffering, the abandonment of friends, the way of the cross—these are the challenges that test the limits of Jesus' trust and acceptance.

Today there is an olive grove at Gethsemane with gnarled and ancient trees that look as though they could have been the silent witnesses to Jesus' sorrowful prayer to the Father that fateful night. Next to the grove is the haunting beauty of the Basilica of the Agony. The dim interior of the church, marked by deep purple windows, evokes the somber grief of those hours. The light focuses on a large rock on which Jesus fell prostrate in his prayerful agony. The fourth-century architects cut away the surrounding rock to isolate the spot. Now the rock is surrounded by a wrought iron crown of thorns. Here countless pilgrims fall upon the rock and pour out their desperate prayers to God. "Thy will be done" is on their lips as they express their personal grief and expectant petitions.

The Gospel accounts show the sharp contrast between Jesus' fervent prayer and the behavior of his disciples. When Jesus returns the first time to find his disciples sleeping, he scolds Peter directly: "So, could you not stay awake with me one hour? Stay awake and pray that you may not come into the time of trial" (Matthew 26:40–41). Even after this explicit imperative, Jesus returns in bitter disappointment to find his disciples sleeping a second time. The cycle then repeats itself a third time, right up to the moment of Jesus' betrayal and arrest. The sequence in which Peter fails to stay awake and pray anticipates Peter's three denials of Jesus still to come.

Jesus' imperative addressed to Peter, "stay awake and pray," is far more than an appeal to be vigilant at that moment. Prayerful anticipation and readiness for the challenges to come must be the constant stance of Jesus' followers. But despite Jesus' warning, Peter does not prepare himself through prayer for his time of trial. Because the disciples are not spiritually vigilant, they are unprepared for the overwhelming crisis of Jesus' passion.

Peter's deepest struggle lies not in his physical fatigue but in the unresolved struggle between the spirit and the flesh: "the spirit indeed is willing, but the flesh is weak" (Matthew 26:41). The spirit inclines us to serve God; the flesh, in its boastful independence from God, is intent on serving itself. In the time of trial, Jesus displays the victory of spirit over flesh, while the disciples exhibit the victory of flesh over spirit. Only with vigilance and prayer can this conflict be resolved in favor of single-minded fidelity to God.

The ceiling of the Basilica of the Agony is deep blue to simulate the night sky. The three large mosaics across the front of the church—the agony of Jesus on the rock in the apse and, on either side, the betrayal by Judas and the arrest of Jesus—reveal the key fateful moments at Gethsemane. A few yards from the church and the olive grove is the Grotto of Gethsemane, memorializing the place where Judas offered Jesus the kiss of betrayal and where Jesus was arrested by the authorities. This cave remains unaltered since the time of Jesus, and Christian worship there dates back to the early centuries.

All four of the Gospels narrate the arrest of Jesus. Judas, knowing where to find Jesus, leads the authorities to him and betrays him. John's Gospel adds that Judas knew the place "because Jesus often met there with his disciples" (John 18:2). The disciples try to prevent the arrest of Jesus by using swords, but Jesus rejects their use of violence. John's Gospel specifies that the sword-wielder is Peter himself.

> Then Simon Peter, who had a sword, drew it, struck the high priest's slave, and cut off his right ear. The slave's name was Malchus. Jesus said to Peter, "Put your sword back into its sheath. Am I not to drink the cup that the Father has given me?" (John 18:10–11)

Again, Peter fails to accept the cross of Jesus, the stumbling block over which he has fallen so many times before. He draws his sword in a violent attempt to change the course of events. Misunderstanding the significance of what lies ahead, both Judas and Peter seek to thwart the designs of God. The efforts of these two men actually work against Jesus, who insists that he is to drink the cup the Father has given him. In this place, where Jesus has met so often with his disciples to instruct them, they fail to understand that Jesus must be lifted up in order to draw all people to himself.

Gethsemane reminds us of Jesus' choice to pour out his whole self for us. His prayers there encourage us not to grow weary and yield to selfish temptations. It urges us to watch and pray, for we don't know when our greatest test of faith will come. In life's agonies, we can turn to our Father who turns the darkness into light and defeat into glory.

Peter Denies Jesus before the Cock Crows

After Jesus was arrested in Gethsemane, his captors brought him to the house of the high priest, Caiaphas. Here Jesus was interrogated by the high priest, mocked and beaten by the guards, and spent the night in prison. Peter followed the arresting party "at a distance" and sat with them around a fire in the courtyard while Jesus was interrogated inside the house. Here Peter denied his master three times before the rooster crowed in the early morning hours of the night.

The house of Caiaphas and Peter's denials are commemorated at the Church of St. Peter in Gallicantu, owned and maintained by the Assumptionist Fathers from France. *Gallicantu* means "cock's crow," and today a golden rooster is mounted in the center of the church's dome. The church is situated at the top of a flight of stone steps dating from the first century, the stairs that Jesus likely trod on his way to and from Gethsemane on the night of his arrest.

While Jesus was on trial in the house of Caiaphas, Peter also found himself on trial. The judge was not the high priest and religious authorities of Jerusalem but a servant girl and the bystanders gathered around the fire that night. Peter's courtroom was the high priest's courtyard, where he testified that he was neither a friend nor a disciple of Jesus. In his moment of trial, Peter denied his relationship with Jesus, a bond that had been the deepest commitment of Peter's life. Although Peter had promised his fidelity to Jesus at the Last

Supper—"Lord, I am ready to go with you to prison and to death!" (Luke 22:33)—he crumpled under his first significant challenge.

The reason Peter denied Jesus was hinted at in Gethsemane when Jesus urged Peter to "stay awake and pray that you may not come into the time of trial." Where Jesus had prayed three times, Peter slept three times. The result of Peter's failure to be vigilant in prayer came later in his three refusals to acknowledge Jesus.

> Now Peter was sitting outside in the courtyard. A servant-girl came to him and said, "You also were with Jesus the Galilean." But he denied it before all of them, saying, "I do not know what you are talking about." When he went out to the porch, another servant-girl saw him, and she said to the bystanders, "This man was with Jesus of Nazareth." Again he denied it with an oath, "I do not know the man." After a little while the bystanders came up and said to Peter, "Certainly you are also one of them, for your accent betrays you." Then he began to curse, and he swore an oath, "I do not know the man!" At that moment the cock crowed. Then Peter remembered what Jesus had said: "Before the cock crows, you will deny me three times." And he went out and wept bitterly. (Matthew 26:69–75)

This dramatic scene builds in intensity as Peter's threefold denial escalates to a powerful climax: "I do not know the man!" Peter must have been startled by his own words as their echo filled the air that dark night. While the drama mounts, Peter gradually retreats—first "sitting outside in the courtyard," then moving "out to the porch," and finally, fleeing the scene after he realizes the horror of what he has done.

The crow of the rooster pierced the darkness of those early hours and startled Peter with the enormity of his denial. He recalled Jesus telling him at the supper that he would deny their relationship three times before the cock would crow. Luke's Gospel heightens the impact of the scene by noting that, at Peter's final denial, "The Lord turned and looked at Peter" (Luke 22:61), then Peter remembered the word of the Lord about the cock's crow.

Often when I read or listen to this account, I think about that look Jesus gave Peter. Presumably the interrogation before Caiaphas had just concluded and Jesus was being led down from the chambers where he had been condemned and humiliated. I can imagine the head of the suffering Lord turning and Jesus' eyes looking straight at Peter. When their eyes met, Peter must have collapsed with grief. Peter projected into the glance of Jesus all his own guilt and became overwhelmed with what he had done. Surely the look of Jesus was a knowing look, given while Peter was still speaking his most strident denial. It also must have been a look of sadness and pain. *You don't know me, Peter?* But certainly the glance of Jesus was, more than anything, a look of tender compassion. It recalled Peter to his better, nobler self. At that moment—the moment of Jesus' look, the moment of the cock's crow—Peter remembered all and he burst into bitter weeping.

Beneath the modern church of St. Peter in Gallicantu are ruins of an earlier Byzantine church, as well as cellars and cisterns from the time of Jesus. One of those cisterns marks the possible place of Jesus' imprisonment during that night of Passover. While Peter went out and wept, Jesus was locked away in a makeshift dungeon where he would spend the night in torturous loneliness. The exterior mosaic of the church depicts Jesus being lowered with ropes into the pit and is captioned by a verse from the psalms: "You have put me in the depths of the Pit" (Psalm 88:6). The whole of this psalm of lament may very well have served as the prayer of Jesus that night.

Despite the tragedy of Peter's denial, his love for Jesus remained. His response to failure made all the difference in whether his personal collapse would lead to defeat or restoration. Unlike Judas, whose response to his betrayal led to the despair of suicide, Peter moved forward by way of the undying love that bound him to his teacher and Messiah. He remembered Jesus' words, wept with remorse, and then repented.

Peter's denial is narrated with minor variations in all four Gospels. The story must have been told by Peter and others as a striking illustration of how grace can triumph over human weakness. In the context of the persecuted church to which the Gospels were written, Peter's story offered hope for the many early Christians who denied knowing Jesus in the crisis of persecution or betrayed their discipleship under threat. Many had renounced their faith under oath in order to save the lives of their families, and they had wept the same bitter tears of remorse. In telling the story of Peter, the evangelists earnestly wanted these Christians to know that even the greatest Christian leader had failed in his discipleship at the critical hour. Through their failure, they could, like Peter, discover the deeper meaning of the cross, the power of the Resurrection, and Christ's forgiving grace.

Questions for Reflection and Group Discussion

1. What is the relationship between Jesus' washing the feet of his disciples and his institution of the Eucharist? Why did he choose both of these actions as his final deeds before his passion?

2. Why did Peter resist letting Jesus wash his feet? What did Peter need to learn from this action of Jesus?

3. Why do you think Peter was so convinced of his inability to fail? Why was he so unprepared for the crisis of Jesus' arrest?

4. Why did Jesus allow Peter to fail? What have you learned from past failures?

5. What "rooster crow" type of event or revelation in your life has helped you realize a failure or flaw in your discipleship?

Colossal statue of St. Peter, St. Peter's Piazza, Vatican City.

Obelisk from Nero's circus, where
Peter was martyred.

Michelangelo's Dome,
St. Peter's Basilica.

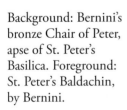

Background: Bernini's
bronze Chair of Peter,
apse of St. Peter's
Basilica. Foreground:
St. Peter's Baldachin,
by Bernini.

Sea of Galilee and boat.

First-century fishing boat discovered in the Sea of Galilee.

Church above the ruins of Peter's House, Capernaum, Mount Tabor.

Church of the Beatitudes above the Sea of Galilee.

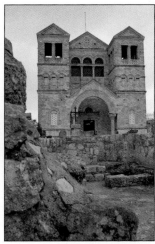

Church of the Transfiguration, Mount Tabor.

Rock on which Jesus prayed, Basilica of the Agony, Gethsemane.

Chapel of the Ascension of Jesus, Mount of Olives.

Church of the Primacy of St. Peter on the Sea of Galilee.

Mamertine Prison, where Peter was chained in Rome.

Relic of Peter's Chains, Church of St. Peter in Chains, Rome.

Clementine Chapel at the Tomb of St. Peter, crypt of
St. Peter's Basilica.

Reliquary of the skulls of Sts. Peter and Paul, St. John
Lateran Basilica.

Mosaic medallions of Peter and his 266 successors, Basilica of St. Paul Outside the Walls.

St. Peter.

Francis and Benedict XVI.

7

Peter Encounters Jesus, the Risen Lord

When we last heard about Peter, he was in the high priest's courtyard as the stark cock's crow pierced the early morning darkness. We are left wondering about how he escaped, where he fled, and how he carried on after the dreadful day of Jesus' crucifixion and death.

After Jesus' death, his body is hastily taken down from the cross, wrapped in a linen cloth, and laid in the tomb on a Friday before sundown, when the Sabbath begins. Not wanting to travel or work on the Sabbath, some are planning to return to the tomb at around sunrise on Sunday (the third day) to complete the customary anointing of Jesus' body for burial.

After the Sabbath has passed, we encounter Peter again in the predawn darkness of "the first day of the week" (John 20:1). He is awakened by the familiar voice of Mary Magdalene telling him that the body of Jesus has been removed from the tomb. Roman troops, religious leaders, grave robbers—someone must have rolled back the stone and carried off his corpse. Peter and the beloved disciple, "the one whom Jesus loved" (John 20:2), hurry toward the tomb.

The disciples don't know it yet, but the whole world has been transformed overnight. Not only is it the first day of a new week; it is the opening day of the new creation. Darkness, sin, death, and hopelessness are conquered. God has reclaimed creation as his own, and humankind and the natural world have been given fresh potential and certain hope. Now Peter and every person must claim that new and everlasting life through the power of the risen Lord.

Disciples are people with good news to share, and the source and center of that good news is the resurrection of Jesus Christ. It is the spark that set the disciples on fire. The simple followers of Jesus, saddened by the crucifixion of their master outside the walls of Jerusalem, are within a short period of time transformed into a jubilant community of believers. And with the burning flame of the truth that he is truly risen, they set the world aflame with penetrating and purifying light.

The Resurrection is not just what happened to Jesus after his death and burial. The Resurrection is the peak of everything that God has been doing throughout the history of salvation. The time of forgiveness, restoration, and victory over sin and death, promised by Israel's prophets and sages for the age to come, has now come upon the earth through Christ's resurrection. In him the new creation, promised for the end of the age, has now begun. We see in him what God has promised as our destiny—resurrection from the dead and the fullness of life forever.

Peter can teach us how to live our present lives in the interval between Christ's resurrection and the day of Christ's coming when the dead will be raised to life. We live now with a mixture of fulfillment and expectation. Jesus Christ is risen, and we can experience his risen presence in countless ways. Yet we wait with eager longing for the fulfillment of the hope he has given us, the fullness of life in God's new creation.

The Basilica of the Holy Sepulcher

When pilgrims arrive at the Basilica of the Holy Sepulcher, located in Jerusalem over the attested burial site of Jesus, often they are surprised that it is so dark and dreary. The church, with the empty tomb at its center, has certainly seen centuries of burning, destruction, looting, and other atrocities within its walls. But at every Easter vigil, when the newly lit flame is passed from the sepulcher to the worshiping assembly gathered in the church, believers experience the deepest purpose of this place. It does not stand as a tomb to be admired by awestruck pilgrims. It is an *empty* space from which the good news of Christ's resurrection is proclaimed to a searching world. The flame is passed from person to person, then from church to church within the city. This ritual of the Easter vigil is re-created in churches all over the world on that solemn night when the Exultet is chanted, the Gospel of the resurrection is proclaimed, new Christians are baptized into his dying and rising, and the resurrected presence of Christ is experienced in Eucharist.

At the center of the basilica's rotunda, beneath its large dome, stands the marble monument containing the rock-hewn tomb of Jesus. If we could deconstruct the entire basilica, with its pillars, altars, lamps, mosaics, and stone flooring, we would find a singular tomb cut away from other burial tombs in an area formerly used as a limestone quarry. In AD 30, the place was simply a garden lying outside the walls of Jerusalem. Deserted and unprotected, it was a suitable place for the crucifixion and burial of criminals.

The doorway of the monument leads to the first chamber, which is called the Chapel of the Angel. Through a second doorway is the chamber containing the marble-covered stone slab on which the body of Jesus was laid to rest. Here pilgrims touch the stone, recite brief prayers, light candles, and recall the gospel proclamation of Easter morning.

Peter Discovers the Empty Tomb

When Peter and the other disciple arrive at the tomb, the sun has begun to rise, so the men can see in the tomb. When Peter enters the tomb, he sees not only the strips of linen that had wrapped Jesus' body but also the cloth that had covered Jesus' face, rolled up and lying to the side. When the beloved disciple enters the tomb, he intuits the significance of the burial wrappings: "he saw and believed" (John 20:8). This does not imply that Peter saw but failed to believe. The beloved disciple is the eyewitness of this Gospel, and the narrative rests on his testimony and is told from his perspective. This anonymous beloved disciple is the model for all other disciples to imitate, the one who gathers the evidence and comes to believe that Jesus is indeed risen.

The careful placement of the grave clothes is the disciples' first compelling clue that something exceedingly significant has happened. It convinces them that the body of Jesus has not been stolen, as Mary Magdalene at first assumed. If the corpse had been taken from the tomb, surely the robbers would not have engaged in the useless task of undressing the body. The arrangement of the linen wrappings and the head cloth lying where the body of Jesus had been laid suggests that an unprecedented divine action has occurred.

This scene at the empty tomb provides a strong contrast to the earlier scene of Lazarus emerging from the tomb. The text says that, at the command of Jesus, "The dead man came out, his hands and feet bound with strips of cloth, and his face wrapped in a cloth" (John 11:44). The raising of Lazarus was a resuscitation of his body, raised again to temporal life, to a physical life that would continue to age. Eventually he would again die and be buried in a tomb.

The resurrection of Jesus was a qualitatively different event. He is risen to new life, to an existence beyond the bounds of space and time, to an eternal life that will never end. The body of Jesus is totally transformed in a way that the writer of the Gospel struggles to describe and that we cannot completely comprehend.

The narrative demonstrates that Peter and the beloved disciple are surprised at what they see and cannot grasp the reality of Jesus' resurrection. The text concludes, "for as yet they did not understand the scripture, that he must rise from the dead" (John 20:9). Later, with the light of the Holy Spirit, Peter will read the ancient Scriptures and better understand the full plan of God. This is the task of the church in every age: to continually read the Old and New Testaments and understand the dying and rising of Jesus as the culmination of God's saving plan.

Jesus Appears to Peter at the Shore of the Sea

In the final scene of John's Gospel, Simon Peter and six other disciples have gathered back at the Sea of Galilee after the traumatic events of Jerusalem. Like thousands of other pilgrims, they have returned home after the Passover festival and resumed their lives. Characteristically, Peter takes the initiative and declares his intention to go fishing. Joined by the others, they all venture out on the sea they know so well, but they fail to make a catch all night.

As the morning breaks, Jesus stands on the shore, but the disciples do not realize it is Jesus because of his transcendent glory. The futility of the disciples' fishing efforts during the night, followed by their tremendous success in the morning light with Jesus present, continues the contrast between darkness and light so typical of this Gospel. Without Jesus, the disciples catch nothing; with his direction, the catch is overwhelming.

It would have been tempting for Peter and his friends to ignore the advice of Jesus. They had been fishing all night and must have been exhausted. But Jesus encourages them to give it another shot and to do it differently this time. This results in an overflowing net: "They were not able to haul it in because there were so many fish." The great catch occurs not just because the fish are there, but because the risen Lord is there with authority and power. The record-breaking catch is the catalyst to recognition. As in the scene at the tomb, the beloved disciple displays insightful recognition and says to Peter, "It is the Lord!" Peter exhibits decisive action: "He jumped into the sea" to swim ashore to Jesus.

As the scene unfolds, we experience a richly beautiful encounter with Jesus on the shore of the sea. Enter this scene with your imagination engaged. Put yourself in the place of Peter. What do you see, hear, smell, taste, and feel? What emotions fill your heart as you encounter the risen Lord?

> When they had gone ashore, they saw a charcoal fire there, with fish on it, and bread. Jesus said to them, "Bring some of the fish that you have just caught." So Simon Peter went aboard and hauled the net ashore, full of large fish, a hundred fifty-three of them; and though there were so many, the net was not torn. Jesus said to them, "Come and have breakfast." Now none of the disciples dared to ask him, "Who are you?" because they knew it was the Lord. Jesus came and took the bread and gave it to them, and did the same with the fish. (John 21:9–13)

The risen Lord has prepared a "charcoal fire" upon which he has placed the roasting fish and bread. Although the burning coals may remind Peter of his denial around the charcoal fire outside the high priest's house, these sparking coals by the sea prepare a meal of communion and reconciliation. How different this fire must have looked to Peter in the light of dawn as the risen Lord invites the disciples to come and eat.

A small church on the shores of the Sea of Galilee commemorates the appearance of the risen Christ to his disciples while they were fishing from their boats. The chapel is built on rock and juts out into the sea. It is called the Church of the Primacy of St. Peter. The flat rock enclosed by the church is called *Mensa Christi*, the "Table of Christ" on which Jesus placed the coals with the bread and the cooked fish. From at least the fourth century, pilgrims have identified this place as the site where the risen Christ prepared a meal for his disciples.

As we read this concluding scene of John's Gospel, we can uncover multiple layers of meaning within it. In addition to its literal sense, the scene expresses the evangelizing mission of the church. The successful fishing expedition symbolizes the church's outreach to the world. The disciples are fishers of men and women, sent out on mission to make new disciples. Because of the presence and direction of the risen Lord, their mission is overwhelmingly successful.

St. Jerome, an ancient commentator on the Gospel, suggests that a hundred fifty-three is the number of species of fish known at the time. So the net full of a hundred fifty-three large fish represents the universality and all-embracing character of the church's mission to evangelize the world. The great catch is the symbolic equivalent of the great commission Jesus gives at the conclusion of Matthew's Gospel: "Go therefore and make disciples of all nations" (Matthew 28:19). This final resurrection appearance at the end of John's Gospel denotes the image of Peter in the early church: the missionary fisher of people under the direction of the risen Lord.

As I lead pilgrims to this small Church of Peter's Primacy on the shore, usually we see waves lapping up onto the rock on which the chapel stands and we hear the sound of the sea. Wading shoeless into the lake, we imagine Peter's excitement at recognizing Jesus, jumping into the water and swimming as fast as he can to meet his master again.

The *Mensa Christi* and the altar of Eucharist in the church connect the meal offered by the risen Jesus at the shore with the sacred meal offered by Christ to his church throughout the ages. The bread and the fish that served as a nourishing meal for his disciples that morning remind us of the loaves and fish with which Jesus had fed the hungry crowds so abundantly. This meal on the beach is also a foretaste of the eucharistic communion that the Lord continually offers to satisfy the hungers and longings of his people gathered as his church.

Jesus Calls Peter to Shepherd His Flock

By making a charcoal fire on the shore, Jesus has, in a sense, re-created the setting in which Peter denied him. The fire reminds Peter of the cold, hostile questioning in the courtyard of the high priest. In the presence of this new fire, which is warm and inviting, Jesus offers Peter another opportunity to affirm his discipleship.

> When they had finished breakfast, Jesus said to Simon Peter, "Simon son of John, do you love me more than these?" He said to him, "Yes, Lord; you know that I love you." Jesus said to him, "Feed my lambs." A second time he said to him, "Simon son of John, do you love me?" He said to him, "Yes, Lord; you know that I love you." Jesus said to him, "Tend my sheep." He said to him the third time, "Simon son of John, do you love me?" Peter felt hurt because he said to him the third time, "Do you love me?" And he said to him, "Lord, you know everything; you know that I love you." Jesus said to him, "Feed my sheep." (John 21:15–17)

Peter had three times denied his relationship with Jesus; now Jesus gives Peter this threefold opportunity to express his love for him. Peter responds more cautiously this time, more humbly aware of his vulnerability and limitations. At long last, Peter has learned that he cannot rely on his own strength and willpower to follow Jesus. Each of his affirmations of love offsets his earlier rejections. In light of this new day, Peter's anguish over his denials is brought to an end as he experiences the healing and reconciling presence of the risen Lord.

Jesus puts to Peter an ambiguous question: "Do you love me more than these?" Is Jesus asking whether Peter loves him more than these fish that they have just caught and eaten—that is, more than his profession? Is he asking if Peter loves him more than he loves these other disciples? Or is Jesus asking whether Peter loves him more than the other disciples love him? All three meanings must be true. Peter must love Jesus more than he loves other people or his fishing business, and he must love Jesus more than the other disciples do, because he must be willing to render extraordinary sacrifice on behalf of his master.

Jesus' threefold question leads to his entrusting Peter with the care of his flock. The triple commissioning expresses Peter's solemn obligation. These sheep, so precious to Jesus, are now given to the care of the sinful yet forgiven Peter. This kind of pastoral care is modeled on that of Jesus, the Good Shepherd. The responsibility given to Peter implies total dedication to the community of faith, guidance through teaching and preaching, and self-giving even to the point of giving his life for them.

> Jesus said to him, "Very truly, I tell you, when you were younger, you used to fasten your own belt and to go wherever you wished. But when you grow old, you will stretch out your hands, and someone else will fasten a belt around you and take you where you do not wish to go." (He said this to indicate the kind of death by which he would glorify God.) After this he said to him, "Follow me."
> (John 21:18–19)

Jesus had said that the Good Shepherd is willing to lay down his life for his sheep. Jesus follows his commission of Peter as shepherd with a prediction of Peter's death. With his freedom taken away, he will be led to the place of execution where he will stretch out his hands in crucifixion. By the time this Gospel was written, the evangelist would have known that Peter died a martyr's death in Rome under the persecution of Nero.

Jesus ends the encounter on the shore by commissioning Peter with the same words that began their relationship: "Follow me." Only now Peter's call to follow Jesus takes on a new and deeper meaning. For the remaining decades of his life, Peter will live in the shadow of the cross, just as Jesus did. He will follow the great Shepherd, tending his flock as shepherd of Christ's followers.

Experience shows that those who are forgiven the most are able to love the most. Peter was able to love with fidelity and commitment because he had failed and had been forgiven. Stripped of his vain pride and self-reliance, Peter was now able to love Jesus with self-sacrificing love. He was able to be the rock, the fisherman, the shepherd of the church that Jesus called him to be.

Questions for Reflection and Group Discussion

1. What led the disciples who saw the empty tomb to believe that Jesus had been resurrected? In what way is the resurrection of Jesus different from the resuscitation of a corpse?

2. Describe the sights and sounds, the aromas, tastes, and textures that come alive as you imagine yourself at the scene of Jesus' appearance at the Sea of Galilee. What are some of the emotions Peter might have experienced when he saw the charcoal fire Jesus had prepared on the sea shore?

3. What are the different levels of meaning we can apply to John's account of Jesus' appearance at the Sea of Galilee?

4. Why did Jesus ask Peter, "Do you love me more than these?" In what way is a call to pastoral ministry based on love for the Lord more than on qualifications?

5. What does Peter's experience of the risen Lord teach you about being a disciple and serving his church?

8

Peter Shepherds the Church in Jerusalem

The movement from the four Gospels to the Acts of the Apostles expresses the transition from the life of Jesus to the early days of his church. In this new stage of saving history, Peter is portrayed in a much more favorable light. His cloud of guilt has lifted, and he is able to serve with confident zeal. In Acts we will watch Peter carrying out the mission entrusted to him by Jesus as the rock, the fisherman, and the shepherd of the church. He will fulfill his multiple roles as spokesperson for the apostles, powerful witness to Jesus Christ, and pastoral leader of the faith community.

Luke, who is the author of both his Gospel and of the Acts of the Apostles, demonstrates the close connection between his two books through the work of the Holy Spirit. The divine Spirit who filled the life of Jesus so completely throughout his earthly life now is given to his church. This Spirit of the risen Jesus empowers the church to announce the good news, in word and deed, and to manifest the reality that Jesus continues to live at the heart of his church. Though established in his heavenly abode, Jesus continues to be present to his community on earth, empowering mediators to act on his behalf to continue the mission he began.

This point of transition from the earthly life of Jesus to the life of his church is dramatized at the top of the Mount of Olives as Acts begins.

> So when they had come together, they asked him, "Lord, is this the time when you will restore the kingdom to Israel?" He replied, "It is not for you to know the times or periods that the Father has set by his own authority. But you will receive power when the Holy Spirit has come upon you; and you will be my witnesses in Jerusalem, in all Judea and Samaria, and to the ends of the earth." When he had said this, as they were watching, he was lifted up, and a cloud took him out of their sight. While he was going and they were gazing up toward heaven, suddenly two men in white robes stood by them. They said, "Men of Galilee, why do you stand looking up toward heaven? This Jesus, who has been taken up from you into heaven, will come in the same way as you saw him go into heaven." (Acts 1:6–11)

Meeting on the Mount with the risen Jesus, the disciples are filled with yearning and hope. They want Jesus to finish the work he has begun, to fulfill his promise to restore God's kingdom. The reply of Jesus is twofold: first, he tells them that they cannot know the timetable for God's plan, which ends their speculation; and second, he tells them that they will be his witnesses in the world. The promised kingdom will be restored in God's own time. In the meantime, they are not to wait idly; rather, they are to be witnesses filled with hope in the promises Jesus has left them.

The key to Acts is provided by the words of the risen Christ: "You will be my witnesses in Jerusalem, in all Judea and Samaria, and to the ends of the earth." This opening-out of the gospel message to a continually wider audience forms the structure of the book, and Peter is shown to be the catalyst of each new stage of the church's expansion. The good news of salvation is offered first to the Jews in Jerusalem, and from there it spreads first to the Samaritans. Then the gospel is brought to the coastal region, to the inhabitants of Lydda, Sharon, and Joppa. The outreach to the Gentiles, the clearest expression of the church's universal mission, begins with Peter entering the home of Cornelius and the conversion of his household. This mission then continues with Paul's journeys throughout Asia Minor, into Greece, and finally to the capital of the empire, the city of Rome.

The thrust and guidance of the church's expanding mission comes from the Holy Spirit. In what is sometimes called a "triple Pentecost," Acts traces the gift of the Spirit first to the Jews, then to the Samaritans, and finally to the Gentiles. At the first Pentecost, many Jewish people who have gathered in Jerusalem accept Peter's invitation to repent, be baptized, and receive the Holy Spirit. As the witness of Jesus' disciples spreads out into Judea and Samaria, many begin accepting the word of God. So the apostles send Peter and John to pray for the Spirit with the Samaritans, and they "laid their hands on them and they received the Holy Spirit" (Acts 8:17). Then the good news expands even to the Gentiles, beginning in the city of Caesarea. When Peter speaks to the crowd, he proclaims that "God shows no partiality" (Acts 10:34)—that people from any nation can experience God's salvation. While he was speaking, "the Holy Spirit fell upon all who heard the word."

This third outpouring of God's Spirit indicates that both Jews and Gentiles could be equally endowed with the gift of the Holy Spirit, thus making way for the expansion of the Christian mission to the whole world. The Spirit drove the church to cross every barrier in proclaiming the gospel, thus guiding the church's mission, first in Jerusalem, then into Judea and Samaria, and finally to the ends of the earth.

When I bring pilgrims to the small circular shrine representing the Ascension of Jesus at the top of the Mount of Olives, I reflect with them on the departure of Jesus. We should avoid being too literal in our understanding of Christ's ascending and descending. The descent of Christ expresses his coming among us in the flesh. The ascent of Christ, the Ascension, represents his leaving this world and entering into the presence of God. It is his transition from flesh to glory that conveys the beginning of a new kind of presence for Jesus—and our hope for his glorious return.

Sometimes people wonder what it would have been like to live with Jesus and follow him during his earthly life. But truly we are able to live more closely with Jesus now than we could have when he walked the earth. The first disciples lived *with* Jesus; but now, in his return to the Father and the sending of his Spirit, we live *in* Jesus. Not only is Jesus deeply and personally present in us, but we are now united to his mission. We must not stand gazing up toward heaven, because we are to be witnesses to Jesus Christ in every place and to everyone.

The two great figures of the Torah and the prophets, Moses and Elijah, each transmitted their "spirit" to their successors at their departure. Because Moses laid his hands on Joshua, his successor, Joshua was filled with the spirit of wisdom and did as God had commanded Moses (Deuteronomy 34:9). Before Elijah ascended into heaven, Elisha, his successor, asked for a double share of his spirit. So when Elijah departed, his spirit became actively present in his successor (2 Kings 2:9, 15). Likewise, as Jesus departs, he promises his Spirit to his disciples. In fact, the two men in white garments may well represent Moses and Elijah, the departed predecessors of Jesus, who appeared with him at the Transfiguration. Of course, Jesus could have stayed longer, or even forever, but he departed in order to leave his work in the hands of his church.

From the top of the Mount of Olives, in light of Christ's Spirit-filled church, I challenge pilgrims to discover the "other side of pilgrimage." Conventional pilgrimage, of course, means going somewhere else to find God in a new way; the other side of pilgrimage means going somewhere else in order to *bring God in a new way to that place*. The call of the risen Christ for us to be his witnesses to the ends of the earth convinces us that now every place can be a holy land. We can witness to the good news and discover the open-ended movements of God's Spirit in the least likely places, and we can bring the presence of God to people and places that wait in darkness for the dawning light of our Risen Lord.

Peter Addresses the Crowd at Pentecost

The amazing event we call Pentecost in Acts 2 marks the baptism of the church with the Spirit and fire. It stirs into flame the grace of Christ's death and resurrection and breathes divine power into the newborn church. This Spirit-filling event happened during the ancient Jewish feast of Pentecost, held fifty days after Passover and also known as the Feast of Weeks (Leviticus 23:15–16). Faithful Jews came to Jerusalem to give offerings and celebrate God's giving of the Torah on Mount Sinai as a covenant-making event. When the new church is born in Jerusalem during Pentecost, God completes his promises to Israel and confirms the *new* covenant. At Sinai, God came down upon the mountain with a terrifying noise and in a mysterious fire. The great sound and fire of the Pentecost event in Jerusalem signify the mysterious presence of God that fills and renews God's people with his Spirit.

The church begins with the coming of the Holy Spirit in the presence of Jews on pilgrimage from all around the world; the Jewish apostles of Jesus announce the good news of Jesus to them all. Luke tells us that everyone was "amazed and perplexed" and they began to ask one another, "What does this mean?" Again, as with all questions of Scripture, this is a query that we all must seek to answer. Through the interplay of Luke the writer and our questioning as the readers, we will be able to articulate and answer this question as we continue to read and listen.

The very first person to speak at Pentecost, in response to the inquiry of the crowd, is Peter. Not only is God creating his people anew, but the Spirit has come to rest on Peter as he begins to speak fearlessly. The same spirit that God blew into the dust to create a human being at the first creation (Genesis 2:7) now breathes life into this once cowardly disciple to create a new man. The same Peter who only a few weeks before could not speak up when his master was on trial now proclaims the message of Christ in the power of the Holy Spirit.

Peter calls on the crowd to listen and begins to speak. He presents Jesus the Nazorean and proclaims what God has done through him. Even though he was crucified as a criminal in Jerusalem, his death was not an arbitrary tragedy; rather, his death and resurrection were necessary according to God's saving will.

> "You that are Israelites, listen to what I have to say: Jesus of Nazareth, a man attested to you by God with deeds of power, wonders, and signs that God did through him among you, as you yourselves know—this man, handed over to you according to the definite plan and foreknowledge of God, you crucified and killed by the hands of those outside the law. But God raised him up, having freed him from death, because it was impossible for him to be held in its power." (Acts 2:22–24)

Peter's speech is replete with quotations and allusions to the Scriptures of Israel. He expresses the early Christian interpretation of the Old Testament in light of the resurrection of Jesus, the key that opens up all the mysteries hidden in Israel's Scriptures. He proclaims that Jesus is the climax of God's saving plan and that his life, death, and resurrection complete the ancient Scriptures. The climax of Peter's speech and the heart of all Christian witness is his declaration that the crucified Jesus is both Lord and Messiah.

The preaching of Peter makes a decisive impact on many people and provokes them to ask another question: "What should we do?" Peter responds with a clear call for a decision.

Peter said to them, "Repent, and be baptized every one of you in the name of Jesus Christ so that your sins may be forgiven; and you will receive the gift of the Holy Spirit. For the promise is for you, for your children, and for all who are far away, everyone whom the Lord our God calls to him." (Acts 2:38–39)

The decision that Peter evokes from the crowd involves both a no and a yes: "Repent" says no to your past life of rejecting God and living for yourselves, and "Be baptized" says yes to God by faith in Jesus Christ. Through repentance and baptism, all who enter this new community of Jesus' disciples will receive forgiveness of sins and the gift of the Holy Spirit.

From his own bitter experience of denying Jesus—and then his renewing experience of Jesus' forgiveness—Peter knows only too well what is needed to receive abundant life. Repentance is not just being sorry; it is an act of radical conversion of mind and heart, a conscious turning toward God to receive the life he offers through Jesus. While repentance is primarily an interior experience, baptism is a public and communal expression of this new life. Baptism in the name of Jesus Christ expresses a person's faith in him and demonstrates that this person has received new life from God.

Peter announces that God calls those in Jerusalem and their children, as well as those who are far away and dispersed among the distant nations. His exhortation is met with enthusiastic acceptance, and thousands are added that day to the community of faith. These form a powerful communal witness to others in the city, so that more and more people come to know Jesus as Messiah and Lord.

Peter Heals the Lame Man at the Temple Gate

These events told in the Acts of the Apostles demonstrate that the ministry of Jesus continues in the apostolic community. The teaching, reconciling, and healing ministry of Jesus extends into the life of the church through the Holy Spirit of Pentecost. Author Luke illustrates this unity and continuity by showing parallels between the Gospel and Acts. Like master, like disciple.

Sometime after Pentecost and the birth of the new church, Peter and John meet up with a man who was lame from birth. The words and gestures of Peter are reminiscent of so many healing accounts of Jesus in the Gospels. It is as if Jesus were still with them, responding to the needs of the sick and afflicted people who came to him for help.

One day Peter and John were going up to the temple at the hour of prayer, at three o'clock in the afternoon. And a man lame from birth was being carried in. People would lay him daily at the gate of the temple called the Beautiful Gate so that he could ask for alms from those entering the temple. When he saw Peter and John about to go into the temple, he asked them for alms. Peter looked intently at him, as did John, and said, "Look at us." And he fixed his attention on them, expecting to receive something from them. But Peter said, "I have no silver or gold, but what I have I give you; in the name of Jesus Christ of Nazareth, stand up and walk." And he took him by the right hand and raised him up; and immediately his feet and ankles were made strong. Jumping up, he stood and began to walk, and he entered the temple with them, walking and leaping and praising God. All the people saw him walking and praising God, and they recognized him as the one who used to sit and ask for alms at the Beautiful Gate of the temple; and they were filled with wonder and amazement at what had happened to him. While he clung to Peter and John, all the people ran together to them in the portico called Solomon's Portico, utterly astonished. (Acts 3:1–11)

For years the man sat every day at the Beautiful Gate, one of the entrances into the temple area, to beg for alms. Because Peter and John regularly entered the temple for afternoon prayers, they must have known the man. Perhaps they had even given him coins; faithful Jews took seriously their responsibility to offer alms.

But on this particular afternoon, the apostles look very intently at him, sensing the Spirit's desire to intervene in this man's life. The lame man gives them his attention, no doubt hoping for financial help. Peter, however, provides him with more than money can buy. His words are emphatic and surprising: "I have no silver or gold, but what I have I give you; in the name of Jesus Christ of Nazareth, stand up and walk."

The miracle is not performed as a feat of magic to amaze the crowds. Just as in the healings of Jesus, the miracle is a visual act that points to a deeper reality. In effect, Peter gives the man new life, portraying what God's salvation can do in the life of anyone who receives it. This story is reminiscent of what the prophet Isaiah said, speaking of the salvation to come: "Then the eyes of the blind shall be opened, and the ears of the deaf unstopped; then the lame shall leap like a deer, and the tongue of the speechless sing for joy" (Isaiah 35:5–6). The lame man walking, leaping, and praising God is a tangible sign of the wholeness and fullness that salvation brings, which God desires for all people.

The healing of the lame man shows us how the emerging church engaged the larger community in which it lived—demonstrating compassion in visible ways to manifest God's saving power. The miracle causes "wonder and amazement" in those who recognize the healed man as the one who used to helplessly ask for alms at the temple gate. Such deeds and responses from the people, as we saw with Jesus' ministry, have the potential to awaken faith and also to create controversy.

As he did at Pentecost, Peter uses the opportunity of the crowd's amazement to focus their attention on Jesus Christ and to rightly place the credit for the healing. The speech Peter delivers expresses the deeper meaning of the miracle account, and it establishes further parallels between Jesus and his apostles. Like Jesus, the apostles are now teaching in the area of the temple; and like Jesus, their teaching is closely connected to the amazing deeds they perform.

Peter's speech makes clear that the power at work in the apostles is not their own: "By faith in his name, his name itself has made this man strong, whom you see and know; and the faith that is through Jesus has given him this perfect health in the presence of all of you" (Acts 3:16). Peter is not in control, manipulating the power he has received. His healing, rather, is an expression of faith and a form of prayer that the will of God be done.

Peter knows that helping his audience understand who Jesus is will help them appreciate what Jesus did. Peter wants to show them how everything that God has done in his servant Jesus is the culmination of a long history of prophecy and expectation. Proclaiming how Jesus is the fulfillment of ancient Scriptures, Peter testifies to the significance of his death and resurrection. Jesus is the Messiah who suffered for his people, the Christ who fulfilled what God foretold through all the prophets. He is "the Holy and Righteous One" who was rejected by those he came to save and handed over to death. But in him, a tragic human "no" was met by God's marvelous "yes" when God raised Jesus from the dead to become "the Author of life."

The name of Jesus is the authority Peter evokes when he preaches. In the power of that name, the sick are healed and sins are forgiven. In this name, Christ's reign in heaven is joined with his church on earth. He alone has the authority to restore people to their original wholeness and create them anew. Peter emphasizes life, not death; repentance, not blame; the forgiving power of God that can raise anyone from the death of sin, just as he raised Jesus from the grave.

Peter's healing of the lame man demonstrates the on-going role of Christ's church in the world. People are broken and wounded, sick and oppressed. Jesus leaves it in the hands of his church—his community of disciples—to be his instruments of healing and compassion today. This healing takes many forms: prayer, medicine, surgery, counseling, forgiveness, and encouragement. Called to heal in the name of Christ, we use whatever means given us to enable others to experience healing as a visible manifestation of the fullness of life God desires for all people.

The Gospel Cannot Be Contained

After the healing of the lame man in the temple courtyard, the religious authorities arrest Peter and John and put them in custody. The temple leaders are threatened by the growing number of people responding to the apostles, now about five thousand believers. Brought in for a judicial inquiry the next day, Peter respectfully addresses his examiners, seeing another opportunity to proclaim the name of Jesus Christ. Without apology, Peter declares what he has done and by whom it was made possible.

> The next day their rulers, elders, and scribes assembled in Jerusalem, with Annas the high priest, Caiaphas, John, and Alexander, and all who were of the high-priestly family. When they had made the prisoners stand in their midst, they inquired, "By what power or by what name did you do this?" Then Peter, filled with the Holy Spirit, said to them, "Rulers of the people and elders, if we are questioned today because of a good deed done to someone who was sick and are asked how this man has been healed, let it be known to all of you, and to all the people of Israel, that this man is standing before you in good health by the name of Jesus Christ of Nazareth, whom you crucified, whom God raised from the dead." (Acts 4:5–10)

Peter, "filled with the Holy Spirit," speaks like a prophet and confronts his listeners with their own accountability. Jesus, whom they crucified and whom God vindicated by raising him to life, is the sole source of all power and healing.

The episode draws a sharp contrast between the Sanhedrin and the apostles. Who holds legitimate leadership over God's people? Is it the Sanhedrin, the leaders in Jerusalem who first rejected Jesus, or is it the apostles, who continue to teach and work wonders in his name? As the book of Acts continues, Luke will show how the apostles become the true leaders of the restored Israel and rule over the twelve tribes, as Jesus had predicted.

After the council deliberates, they know they cannot punish the apostles. As evidence of the power of Jesus' resurrection at work through the apostles, the healed man stands before them. Instead, they try to intimidate the apostles and warn them never to speak to anyone again in the name of Jesus. Will their orders prevail? We can already guess the answer.

This first indication of persecution against the apostles demonstrates that God has not called them to proclaim a gospel without sacrifice. They follow Jesus and are sent out in imitation of the one who suffered and experienced the rejection of many. These Spirit-filled apostles will not be deterred, neither by their own fear nor by the threats of others. In response to the order to cease speaking in the name of Jesus, Peter and John reply, "Whether it is right in God's sight to listen to you rather than to God, you must judge; for we cannot keep from speaking about what we have seen and heard" (Acts 4:19–20).

The Power and Authority of Christ Working through Peter

In the Acts of the Apostles we see several characteristics of the community of disciples. The believers form a learning church, a loving church, a worshiping church, and an evangelizing church. They find their unity in the teachings of the apostles, they hold their possessions in common to serve the needy, they celebrate the breaking of the bread and the prayers, and they proclaim the gospel of Jesus Christ in word and deed. The quality of their life together earns them the good favor of those outside the community. The church's witness is infectious, and their numbers grow steadily as God converts hearts and leads many to salvation.

When Peter and John are released, they return to the community of disciples and report what the authorities said to them. In response to the warning of the religious leaders to cease preaching or teaching in the name of Jesus, the community raises their voices in prayer. They pray neither to avoid maltreatment nor for God's punishment on their persecutors but for the strength to do God's will and to preach the message boldly in the midst of persecution.

> "And now, Lord, look at their threats, and grant to your servants to speak your word with all boldness, while you stretch out your hand to heal, and signs and wonders are performed through the name of your holy servant Jesus." (Acts 4:29–30)

The preaching of the church and the visible deeds of God go hand in hand, each confirming and upholding the other. They express their dependence on God and their desire only to carry out the mission to which they have been called.

As the healing ministry of Jesus continues in the work of his church, the apostles bring physical and spiritual healing to people, performing "signs and wonders" on behalf of the sick and the possessed. In a culture that often links sin with suffering and that regards sick persons as under the power of evil spirits, the early church extends compassion and welcome to the sick. It does so in confidence that Jesus' death and resurrection has broken the power of the Evil One. There is nothing to fear from contact with outcasts, and the sick and suffering are God's beloved ones.

During the earthly life of Jesus, Peter had followed Jesus from town to town, watching him cure the sick and heal the hopeless from despair. Now the crowds are following Peter around the streets of Jerusalem, bringing their sick for healing.

> Yet more than ever believers were added to the Lord, great numbers of both men and women, so that they even carried out the sick into the streets, and laid them on cots and mats, in order that Peter's shadow might fall on some of them as he came by. A great number of people would also gather from the towns around Jerusalem, bringing the sick and those tormented by unclean spirits, and they were all cured. (Acts 5:14–16)

The people's hope that Peter's shadow might fall on the sick demonstrates the extent of Christ's power working through him. It is not necessarily the direct touch and awareness of Peter that brings healing to people's lives. Their cures occur, rather, through faith in Jesus that the presence of Peter inspires within them. Peter has become so transformed through God's Spirit working in him that his closeness conveys to people something of the presence of Jesus.

The growth and success of the church are remarkable. Despite the continual arrest and imprisonment of the apostles, their preaching cannot be contained. The greater the authorities' efforts to prevent the apostles from proclaiming the good news of Jesus, the more effective their witness becomes. The distinguished religious council of Jerusalem is continually embarrassed and perplexed that, despite all the precautions they take, the apostles are back again and again, preaching in the temple courts and on the streets of the city.

The Sanhedrin is powerless to stop the spread of God's word as the apostles follow the divine mandate to continue preaching. The bafflement of the religious leaders contrasts starkly with the wondrous deeds and fearless teaching of the apostles, who remain undaunted by threats, arrests, beatings, and imprisonment. It is clearer than ever that the apostles of Jesus are the true rulers of the restored Israel. Nothing will be able to stop the advance of the gospel. The opposition may be able to persecute the church, but they will never defeat the community of those who believe in the Resurrection.

The impulsive abruptness that characterized Peter during the ministry of Jesus has now become courageous boldness through the transformation that faith offers. Willing now to suffer and die for the sake of the gospel, his life illustrates the power of forgiveness and the transformation offered through the risen Christ. Called before the highest authorities in Jerusalem, Peter and the apostles refuse to obey their order to be silent about Jesus. Ordered to cease preaching, Peter defiantly responds, "We must obey God rather than any human authority" (Acts 5:29). Standing before the council more as their judge than their victim, Peter the fisherman powerfully proclaims the salvation given by Jesus Christ.

Peter shows us that the experience of faith in Jesus as Lord implies a vocation to evangelize, to pass on the good news to others. So he makes it plain to the authorities who persecute the apostles that they have no other option than to place their divine calling before all other human commands and prohibitions. The persecution of the church in Jerusalem leads to the expansion of Christianity into the regions around the city. This same pattern continues for the church throughout history. The more the church is silenced, oppressed, and persecuted, the more it grows and the stronger it becomes. Truly the gospel cannot be contained.

Questions for Reflection and Group Discussion

1. What does the transformation of Peter that happened between Christ's Passion and the Day of Pentecost say to you about the forgiving power of Jesus and the anointing power of his Spirit?

2. What does Peter do for the lame man besides enabling him to walk? Why is Peter able to work wonders?

3. In what ways can you imitate Peter in bringing healing to others in the name of Jesus?

4. As in the life of Jesus, the preaching and the deeds of Peter are often intertwined. Why are words and actions bound together in the ministry of Christ's church?

5. Through the Holy Spirit, the same power and courage given to Peter is available to us. When have you felt empowered to do something that you felt completely inadequate to do?

9

Peter Opens the Church to Its Universal Mission

As the maltreatment of the church in Jerusalem intensifies, the disciples begin to expand the community of believers to the nearby towns and the surrounding regions. The persecution of the church, intended to suppress the church's growth, has the opposite effect. The dispersion of the church beyond Jerusalem leads to a widening proclamation of the gospel.

After the stoning of Stephen and the beginning of the persecution led by Saul, the book of Acts reports the dispersion of believers throughout the area.

> That day a severe persecution began against the church in Jerusalem, and all except the apostles were scattered throughout the countryside of Judea and Samaria. . . . Now those who were scattered went from place to place, proclaiming the word. (Acts 8:1, 4)

The scattered seed of God's word bears an increasingly wide harvest of faith. Luke is describing the growth of the church, just as the risen Jesus had predicted: "You will be my witnesses in Jerusalem, in all Judea and Samaria, and to the ends of the earth" (Acts 1:8).

Peter first travels to Samaria, an area to the north of Jerusalem, midway between Judea and Galilee. The outreach to the Samaritans continues the mission of Jesus himself, who encountered the Samaritan woman at the well and brought her townspeople to believe in him as Savior of the world. These Samaritans were held in contempt by the Jews of Jerusalem because of their mixed ancestry and infidelity to the Jewish covenant. But the church's understanding of the boundaries of God's people is changing rapidly. No one would ever have thought that the despised Samaritans would become disciples of the Jewish Messiah. But thanks to missionaries like Philip, many came to believe in the gospel and were baptized (Acts 8:4–5).

In order to demonstrate the continuity between the work of the first missionaries to Samaria and the ministry of the apostles in Jerusalem, Peter and John are sent to confirm the faith and baptisms of these new believers. The prayers of the apostles and the laying on of hands provide a physical and sacramental link between the apostles and the expanding church.

> Now when the apostles at Jerusalem heard that Samaria had accepted the word of God, they sent Peter and John to them. The two went down and prayed for them that they might receive the Holy Spirit (for as yet the Spirit had not come upon any of them; they had only been baptized in the name of the Lord Jesus). Then Peter and John laid their hands on them, and they received the Holy Spirit. (Acts 8:14–17)

Peter and John embrace the Samaritans as brothers and sisters in the newly expanding family of God. The Samaritans receive the Holy Spirit, and so they share with the other disciples in the joy, courage, confidence, and self-dedication that mark those who believe the gospel and are anointed by the Spirit.

Among the more curious characters in the early church is a Samaritan named Simon the magician. He had so amazed the people by his sorcery that they believed his power to be divine. When this Simon sees the power of the Spirit communicated by the apostles through the laying on of hands, he offers to purchase this power for himself with money. But Peter rebukes him in the harshest way and urges him to repent.

> Peter said to him, "May your silver perish with you, because you thought you could obtain God's gift with money! You have no part or share in this, for your heart is not right before God. Repent therefore of this wickedness of yours, and pray to the Lord that, if possible, the intent of your heart may be forgiven you. For I see that you are in the gall of bitterness and the chains of wickedness." (Acts 8:20–23)

Peter's severe admonition demonstrates that Christianity has nothing to do with magic. The Holy Spirit cannot be manipulated and divine power cannot be bought. The sin of simony—paying for position and influence in the church—is named after this Simon. By highlighting this sin, Peter teaches that the work of the Holy Spirit must be received as a benevolent act and a grace from God. After Peter's admonishment, Simon requests the prayers of the community, offering us hope that he will repent of his wickedness, trust in God's grace, and be forgiven.

Peter's Pastoral Visit to the Mediterranean Coast

Peter made frequent pastoral visits to the communities of believers outside Jerusalem. Next in the Acts account, we find him going west from Jerusalem toward the Mediterranean Sea. He is traveling on the borders of the Jewish homeland and closer to the wider world of the Gentiles. He first comes to the city of Lydda, about a day's journey west of Jerusalem. Today, this site is the location of Israel's international airport. The city is within the Plain of Sharon, the coastal plain known for its beautiful wildflowers, especially the rose of Sharon.

In Lydda, Peter visits the community of believers and is introduced to a paralytic named Aeneas.

Now as Peter went here and there among all the believers, he came down also to the saints living in Lydda. There he found a man named Aeneas, who had been bedridden for eight years, for he was paralyzed. Peter said to him, "Aeneas, Jesus Christ heals you; get up and make your bed!" And immediately he got up. And all the residents of Lydda and Sharon saw him and turned to the Lord. (Acts 9:32–35)

Peter tells him to arise, making it clear that Peter is the mediator of divine healing but that the risen Jesus is the healer. Peter's instruction, "get up and make your bed," shows that Aeneas is restored to health and can now care for himself. With his new vitality, he becomes a witness to what Jesus can do, as many residents of the region become believers.

Peter next travels to Joppa, another day's journey westward. Joppa became the port city for Jerusalem under King Solomon, where he received the cedars from Lebanon brought on great rafts for building the temple. Solomon also received guests there from foreign lands. At the time of Jesus and the early church, Joppa was still a significant port, but its importance had been eclipsed by the maritime city of Caesarea.

At Joppa, a disciple named Tabitha was known for her good works and charitable giving. She had become sick and died, causing deep grief to the church there. Hearing that Peter is in nearby Lydda, the disciples send emissaries to bring Peter to Tabitha. When Peter arrives at the upstairs room where her body lies, the widows are weeping and showing him the clothing she made for them.

Peter put all of them outside, and then he knelt down and prayed. He turned to the body and said, "Tabitha, get up." Then she opened her eyes, and seeing Peter, she sat up. He gave her his hand and helped her up. Then calling the saints and widows, he showed her to be alive. This became known throughout Joppa, and many believed in the Lord. Meanwhile he stayed in Joppa for some time with a certain Simon, a tanner. (Acts 9:40–43)

When Tabitha opens her eyes, Peter helps her up. Peter calls the community together and presents her alive, and the word spreads and many more believe in the Lord.

Luke's writings show clear parallels between the healing acts of Jesus in his Gospel and those of Peter in the book of Acts. The healing of Aeneas is similar to Jesus' cure of the paralytic. Jesus commanded the healed man to get up, pick up his bed, and go home, a similar indication that the man was then able to care for himself (Luke 5:24). Peter's resuscitation of Tabitha echoes a similar account in the Gospel. At the raising of Jairus's daughter, Jesus cleared the room and commanded the girl to get up (Luke 8:54–55). Peter's word of command in Aramaic would have been, "Tabitha, cumi," which is only slightly different from the well-known words of Jesus to the young girl, "Talitha, cumi." These parallels are no coincidence. Peter's ministry demonstrates that Jesus is still powerfully at work in his church.

The Visions of Peter and Cornelius

The disciples of Jesus continue breaking down the barriers that divide people. Divisions between rich and poor, slave and free, male and female are overcome in the new way of life inspired by Jesus. The first-century church seems to be a model of respectful equality. Now the final barrier, the most difficult, is about to be destroyed. The racial, cultural, and religious wall that divides Jews and Gentiles will be the supreme test of the power of God's Spirit at work among the early Christians. The reception of the Gentiles into the church will initiate the fundamental step of bringing Christianity from an ethnic religion of Jews to a truly universal faith.

To prepare Peter to be the channel for this monumental breakthrough, God offers Peter a symbolic vision to reveal the divine will. One day while Peter is staying at the house of Simon the tanner in Joppa, he goes up to the roof at about noon to pray.

He became hungry and wanted something to eat; and while it was being prepared, he fell into a trance. He saw the heaven opened and something like a large sheet coming down, being lowered to the ground by its four corners. In it were all kinds of four-footed creatures and reptiles and birds of the air. Then he heard a voice saying, "Get up, Peter; kill and eat." But Peter said, "By no means, Lord; for I have never eaten anything that is profane or unclean." The voice said to him again, a second time, "What God has made clean, you must not call profane." This happened three times, and the thing was suddenly taken up to heaven. (Acts 10:10–16)

The Jewish dietary prohibitions specified in Leviticus 11 distinguish between animals that may be eaten, known as "clean," and animals that may not be eaten, known as "unclean." So, when the heavenly voice says of the creatures shown, "kill and eat," Peter protests, saying that he has never eaten anything profane or unclean. But, pressing against Peter's Jewish practice, the heavenly voice insists, "What God has made clean, you must not call profane."

The same prohibitions that have separated animals into clean and unclean have also divided people from one another. Peter realizes that his symbolic vision is not only about food laws but also about fellowship and acceptance. It expresses God's will to remove the barriers that divide Jews and Gentiles. If God is making unclean food clean, then Jewish Christians may share table fellowship with Gentiles and cross the barriers that before now prevented the gospel from being brought to all people.

Meanwhile, a man named Cornelius has a parallel vision in the city of Caesarea, a day's journey north of Joppa. Cornelius is a military officer of the Roman army. As such, he represents the oppressive empire that has held Israel in subjugation. He is stationed in the seacoast city that serves as capital of the Roman forces. Cornelius truly is an outsider. Although he has lived devoutly, praying often and giving alms generously, he is in fact a Gentile—an outsider with whom a Jew would never associate. But on this day, Cornelius has a vision in which he sees an angel of God coming to him and calling his name.

One afternoon at about three o'clock he had a vision in which he clearly saw an angel of God coming in and saying to him, "Cornelius." He stared at him in terror and said, "What is it, Lord?" He answered, "Your prayers and your alms have ascended as a memorial before God. Now send men to Joppa for a certain Simon who is called Peter; he is lodging with Simon, a tanner, whose house is by the seaside." (Acts 10:3–6)

Through their parallel visions, God draws Peter and Cornelius together. When the men sent by Cornelius arrive in Joppa and explain to Peter the purpose of their mission, Peter begins to understand the meaning and purpose of his vision. He hosts the men overnight in preparation for their journey the next day to Caesarea. Meanwhile, Cornelius invites his relatives and friends to his own house to hear what Peter will say.

As the narrative unfolds, the action shuttles back and forth between Peter and Cornelius, emphasizing the dual nature of the account. This is the story of two conversions: Peter's and Cornelius's. Each man must change if the saving plan of God for all people is to go forward. Clearly God is working from both ends: preparing Cornelius to receive the good news of Jesus Christ and preparing Peter to offer it to him. God is breaking down the barriers that for so long have been assumed to be God's will.

Arriving the next day at Caesarea, Peter takes the first step in opening the church to the Gentiles by walking through the open door of Cornelius's home. Cornelius considers Peter a messenger from God and immediately falls at his feet to worship him. But Peter graciously instructs Cornelius, "Stand up, I am only a mortal." Peter knows that whatever he has to offer this Gentile officer does not come from himself.

Peter then tells the assembled crowd that entering the home of a Gentile is not customary Jewish practice. Jews had erected firm barriers against Gentiles because of the need to maintain the purity of their belief and worship and to prevent Jewish life from being infiltrated by pagan doctrines and practices. Yet Peter goes on to explain that God has rearranged his understanding of what is clean and unclean: "God has shown me that I should not call anyone profane or unclean." Peter realizes that his vision was not only about clean and unclean animals but also about people. He knows that the invitation to eat the forbidden animals was also an exhortation to go and stay at the house of Cornelius. Peter now understands that such barriers between Jews and Gentiles no longer serve their original purpose, because God is bringing about a new age of salvation for all.

When Jesus gave Peter the authority to lead his church, Jesus enabled him to guide the practices of the community in ways that would have far-reaching consequences. This critical section of Acts shows that Peter is indeed the authoritative guide within the early church as he is moved by the assurance of God's Spirit to open the way of faith to the Gentiles. Though the apostolic mission to all parts of the world will soon be led by Paul, the apostle to the Gentiles, this narrative makes it clear that Peter was the inaugurator of this mission. Paul's missionary activity can take place only after Peter's inspired and decisive action opens the door.

Peter Proclaims the Gospel to the Gentiles

After reading the parallel stories of Peter and Cornelius, we have high expectations when Peter addresses the people in Cornelius's household. This is the last example of Peter's preaching offered in Acts, and it is his only address to a Gentile audience. But through this encounter Peter shows how the gospel is to be extended beyond the Jewish people to whom it was originally offered, to make salvation in Christ available to every believer.

> Then Peter began to speak to them: "I truly understand that God shows no partiality, but in every nation anyone who fears him and does what is right is acceptable to him. You know the message he sent to the people of Israel, preaching peace by Jesus Christ—he is Lord of all. That message spread throughout Judea, beginning in Galilee after the baptism that John announced: how God anointed Jesus of Nazareth with the Holy Spirit and with power; how he went about doing good and healing all who were oppressed by the devil, for God was with him. We are witnesses to all that he did both in Judea and in Jerusalem. They put him to death by hanging him on a tree; but God raised him on the third day and allowed him to appear, not to all the people but to us who were chosen by God as witnesses, and who ate and drank with him after he rose from the dead. He commanded us to preach to the people and to testify that he is the one ordained by God as judge of the living and the dead. All the prophets testify about him that everyone who believes in him receives forgiveness of sins through his name." (Acts 10:34–43)

Peter begins his address with a stunning proclamation: "I truly understand that God shows no partiality." God treats everyone on the same basis, and people from every nation have the same potential access to God. Peter highlights only two characteristics of the person who is acceptable to God: "anyone who fears him and does what is right." Those who treat God with reverence and people who do justice are ready for the saving revelation of God through Jesus Christ.

As Peter summarizes the essentials of the Christian message, he emphasizes that Jesus is "Lord of all," to Jew and Gentile alike. He is expressing the universal will of the risen Christ—that the message of salvation be preached from Jerusalem to all the nations. This great commission that Jesus gave his disciples is beginning to be realized as the news extends beyond Jerusalem.

The proclamation of the good news can be meaningless words for a person who is not ready to receive it. It is the message of salvation only for a person who is searching and who realizes the need for God. Cornelius had been seeking God for a long time. He had already begun to pray and to do good for those in need. God had been preparing his mind and heart for the message he receives now from Peter. Through the preached gospel, Cornelius has gone from open seeker to confirmed believer.

While Peter is still speaking, proclaiming forgiveness of sins to everyone who believes, the Holy Spirit comes upon Cornelius and the other Gentiles who are listening to Peter. The Jews who came with Peter are amazed that the gift of the Holy Spirit has been poured out even on the Gentiles. The coming of God's promised Spirit is the sign of the new era, and this event has rightly been called the Pentecost of the Gentile world.

Peter understands the significance of the moment, and he instructs that these Gentiles be baptized in the name of Jesus Christ. Jews and Gentiles are equal in Christ; their need and God's answer to that need are the same. Peter is the primary instrument of God's epoch-making work, showing that the Gentiles too are chosen for salvation, baptism, and membership in Christ's church. The gospel is now ready to go out into the entire world.

The Coastal Cities of Peter's Expanding Ministry

Pilgrims arriving from Ben Gurion International Airport often begin their Holy Land tour with the cities of the Mediterranean coast. I prefer to visit these coastal sites at the end of the trip because they are the places from which the gospel was launched westward throughout the Roman Empire. From the port cities of Jaffa and Caesarea Maritima the gospel message was taken by Peter, Paul, and other missionaries into Asia Minor, Greece, and Italy. And it was from these ports that Peter sailed to Rome, where he served the church until the end of his life.

Jaffa, (or Joppa) is the more ancient port. Its hilltop offers a commanding view of the coastline; in ancient times it was important both militarily and commercially. After the city was conquered by King David and Solomon, it became the critical port for the kingdom. Here the story of Jonah comes alive. In that story, the prophet left on a ship from this harbor to escape God's call that he preach in Nineveh.

The best-known rooftop in modern-day Jaffa, thanks to Peter's vision, belongs to the house of Simon the tanner. It is recognizable by the lighthouse, installed in the nineteenth century to guide ships and fishing vessels past Jaffa's rocky shoals. Members of an Armenian Christian family own the house and operated the lighthouse for generations. Of course, the present house is not the original house from the first century, but local tradition identifies it as the location where Peter was praying when he experienced his transforming vision.

In the middle of the city sits the Church of St. Peter. A Franciscan church, it was first built in the seventeenth century and has been rebuilt twice. Back in the days when pilgrims arrived by ship, its tall bell tower let them know that their long voyage was almost over. The Franciscans had a guesthouse to welcome pilgrims off the boats. The church memorializes Peter's vision with a painting of his roof-top experience above the altar. It also commemorates the raising of Tabitha by Peter. The nearby Russian Orthodox church claims the tomb of Tabitha.

Here in this city we can reflect on the wideness of God's saving love. God taught the ancient Israelites about God's care for the hated people of Nineveh through the story of Jonah the prophet. Peter learned of God's love for the Gentiles through his vision and encounter with Cornelius. Here at this gateway to the world, we can ask God to give us the grace to see people with his eyes, to embrace with compassion people who are different from us. We can pray to have the heart of an evangelizer, to share the good news we have received with all who are seeking God.

North of Jaffa, along the coastal Plain of Sharon, stands the ruins of Caesarea. This ancient city is about halfway between Jaffa and the tip of the Mount Carmel range. It was built by Herod the Great and called Caesarea Maritima to distinguish it from other cities dedicated to the Roman Caesar. Here Herod built a deep sea harbor, including wide roads, markets, public baths, temples to Rome and Augustus, a hippodrome, and a theater. A double aqueduct brought water from springs at the foot of Mount Carmel. Herod also built his palace on a promontory jutting out into the sea. Most of these ancient structures have been excavated and can still be seen in ruins today.

Caesarea Maritima was the civilian and military capital of the Roman province of Judea and served as the official residence of the Roman procurators. During the excavations, the Pilate Stone was uncovered, the only archaeological find of a first-century Roman inscription mentioning the name Pontius Pilatus, the prefect by whose orders Jesus was crucified. Pilate held his primary residence in Caesarea and went to Jerusalem only during the Jewish feasts when tensions ran high there.

Caesarea later became a prominent city during the Byzantine and Crusader periods. The city walls, Crusader castle, and cathedral can still be seen today. In the early centuries of Christianity, the theological school of Caesarea had the reputation for having the most extensive library of the time. Patristic writers such as Gregory Nazianzus, Basil the Great, Jerome, and others came to study here.

After viewing the extensive ruins of Caesarea, I like to gather pilgrims in the ancient Roman theater, which faces the Mediterranean Sea. I tell the story of Peter and Cornelius and the way God opened the way for the Gentiles. Then I look out toward the Sea and reflect on the fact that this was the exit port for spreading the faith. From this harbor both Peter and Paul, and many other early evangelists, brought the gospel to the world.

Christ's Call to Evangelize

In the first century, the sea represented a barrier, especially for Jewish people. Their life was centered on the Promised Land, and they had a greater desire to come to the land than to leave it. But Jesus told his disciples to go out and make disciples of all the nations. He called them to be his witnesses to the ends of the earth. According to one legend, after Jesus gave them the great commission, the apostles got out a map of the world and chose which countries each would evangelize.

Because all Christian missions to the nations left from Caesarea, this place reminds me most forcefully of the essential Christian call to evangelize. Although this city was built during the Roman Empire that honored Caesar as the world's lord and savior, believers who left from this harbor to bring good news to the nations proclaimed that Jesus is the true Lord and the Savior of the world. They knew that he called them to cross boundaries and overcome barriers so that everyone could experience the forgiveness and divine life he offers.

The Acts of the Apostles is an open-ended book. This means that the work does not have a definitive conclusion. It is written in such a way that it draws its readers into the church's mission and helps them realize that the action of the story continues in their own lives. The opening-out of the gospel message to a continually wider audience forms the structure of the book. We've seen the ministry of Peter as he brings the good news first to Samaria, then to the coastal regions of Lydda, Sharon, and Joppa, and finally to the clearest expression of the church's universal mission: the conversion and baptism of Cornelius and his whole household in Caesarea. But the inner vitality for this outreach issues from the Holy Spirit, the same divine Spirit who directs the church today.

In a homily addressed to the new ecclesial movements on the Feast of Pentecost, Pope Francis spoke about this outward-directed dynamism of the Holy Spirit.

> The Holy Spirit draws us into the mystery of the living God and saves us from the threat of a church which is Gnostic and self-referential, closed in on herself; he impels us to open the doors and go forth to proclaim and bear witness to the good news of the gospel, to communicate the joy of faith, the encounter with Christ. The Holy Spirit is the soul of mission. The events that took place in Jerusalem almost two thousand years ago are not something far removed from us; they are events which affect us and become a lived experience in each of us. The Pentecost of the Upper Room in Jerusalem is the beginning, a beginning which endures. The Holy Spirit is the supreme gift of the risen Christ to his apostles, yet he wants that gift to reach everyone.[4]

Israel's coastal plain is the historical land bridge between Europe, Asia, and Africa. Even the geography of salvation expresses God's will that the gospel be brought to all the nations. Clearly the Holy Spirit is the animating energy of the church's evangelization. Whether today's pilgrims return home from the Holy Land through the port cities of Jaffa or Caesarea, or fly from the international airport at ancient Lydda, pilgrims must bring with them the challenge to evangelize. With the Spirit of God we must be about the business of tearing down barriers that divide people, of crossing boundaries of prejudice and bias that prevent the gospel from being truly universal today. We are called always to go to new places and new people, bringing to them the forgiving and saving power of Christ's love.

Questions for Reflection and Group Discussion

1. Why does the book of Acts echo the miracles of Jesus in the works of Peter?

2. What do you see as the primary meaning of Peter's noon-time vision on the rooftop? What did it teach him?

3. In what ways does God draw both Peter and Cornelius together? How does God convert both of their hearts in the process?

4. Peter began his address to the household of Cornelius by saying, "I truly understand that God shows no partiality." When has a cultural or religious belief of yours been questioned, challenged, or altered by further evidence or experience?

5. How does God lead Peter to cross boundaries and break down barriers for the sake of spreading the gospel? What walls prevent the gospel from being truly universal today?

10

Peter Set Free to Become the Worldwide Fisherman and Shepherd

In the years after Peter opened the church to Gentiles, the persecution of the church in Jerusalem grew intense. This persecution was no longer fueled only by the religious authorities of the city, but by the civil government of Herod. This tyrant was Herod Agrippa, the grandson of Herod the Great who cruelly murdered Jewish children around the time of Jesus' birth. Herod Agrippa ruled over Judea from AD 41–44. He wanted to annihilate the Christian movement by striking at its highest leadership.

Herod first arrested James, the brother of John. These two brothers had formed, along with Peter, the inner circle of Jesus' closest disciples. James was the first apostle to die, and John would be the last. James was killed "with the sword"—that is, beheaded like John the Baptist. Jews viewed this manner of death as utterly appalling. Perhaps Herod hoped that by killing James he would frighten the other leaders into silence.

When the religious leaders of Jerusalem praised Herod for moving against the church and putting James to death, he singled out Peter as his next target. The community of believers was stunned by James's execution, so when Peter was taken, there was great distress. Peter's arrest and imprisonment occurred during the seven-day feast of Passover, when Jerusalem was crowded with pilgrims (Acts 12:3). Herod planned to bring Peter before the people after Passover to face judgment. He wanted to make a public spectacle of Peter's trial and execution.

Herod put Peter under heavy guard. He assigned no fewer than sixteen soldiers—four quaternions with four men each. Each squad took guard duty for three hours while the others slept. One soldier was chained to each of Peter's arms, and two others guarded the door. Meanwhile, the church prayed fervently that God would spare Peter's life. To lose the chief apostle would have been devastating. The church needed his guidance and strength.

Peter surely expected to be executed. He had been imprisoned for several days in the Antonia Fortress on the north side of the temple mount. He knew that the last night before his scheduled judgment and execution had arrived.

Yet he was sleeping peacefully, obviously trusting that God would be glorified through his death. At the last moment, God acted through the ministry of an angel to rescue him. With a shining light, God rescued Peter from the darkness and liberated him from imminent death. Luke tells the story in Acts.

> The very night before Herod was going to bring him out, Peter, bound with two chains, was sleeping between two soldiers, while guards in front of the door were keeping watch over the prison. Suddenly an angel of the Lord appeared and a light shone in the cell. He tapped Peter on the side and woke him, saying, "Get up quickly." And the chains fell off his wrists. The angel said to him, "Fasten your belt and put on your sandals." He did so. Then he said to him, "Wrap your cloak around you and follow me." Peter went out and followed him; he did not realize that what was happening with the angel's help was real; he thought he was seeing a vision. After they had passed the first and the second guard, they came before the iron

gate leading into the city. It opened for them of its own accord, and they went outside and walked along a lane, when suddenly the angel left him. (Acts 12:6–10)

Peter is taken by surprise. The chains fall off his wrists, and he is set free. He is not sure what is happening. But when he sees the iron gate open of its own accord and finds himself back on the city streets, he knows that God is at work. He realizes that God has indeed delivered him from captivity.

When Peter emerges from the prison alive, he goes off to tell the disciples the good news. He arrives at the house where the disciples are meeting and knocks on the door. With comic detail, the writer describes how the servant girl, Rhoda, is so excited at realizing it is Peter that she forgets to open the door for him. Instead, she rushes off to tell the community of believers gathered inside. While they argue for a while over Rhoda's sanity, Peter continues to knock at the door. He has a harder time getting into the house of the believing community than he had getting out of prison. An angel led him out of Herod's cell, but he cannot get through the locked gate of the disciples. When finally he is allowed in the house, Peter tells the astonished crowd what happened.

There are clear parallels between Peter's ordeal and Jesus' passion and resurrection. Both occur at Passover. Peter's emergence from prison resembles Jesus' emergence from the tomb; and in both cases the disciples fail to believe the good news brought by women. Peter's escape from prison demonstrates that the resurrection of Jesus continues to empower his apostles. The pattern of God's action in Jesus remains the pattern for God's action in his followers. In the midst of hardship, God continues to offer new life.

The writer makes us smile as we try to imagine the guards' confusion the next morning. Each blaming the other, they are flabbergasted by the empty chains beside them. Quite a commotion is raised as Herod searches for Peter and cannot find his prized prisoner. The writer contrasts the scene of the church gathered in the house with that of the baffled guards in the prison. The one is a scene of bewildered joy and gratitude, the other a scene of revenge and punishment. While the Christians praise God for Peter's deliverance, Herod orders that all the prison guards be put to death.

The Fallen Chains of Peter

The prisons of the ancient world were not built to code, as are many jails today. The dungeon holding Peter was dark and dank. The watch level was maximum security. A double chain fastened the prisoner to two soldiers, one on each side of him. The iron gate was securely fastened with Roman guards at each station. Herod had made arrangements for an imposing spectacle that would earn the people's applause. With the morning light, he would bring his victim out of his cell for a showy judgment and a sentence of death.

Peter was sleeping between his guards, seeking some minimal comfort while his arms were bound in the metal chains. And a little way off, the church was keeping solemn watch and pouring forth intense prayers through the night. There was no foolish escape plan, no plot unfolding for a dramatic rescue. Peter and the church he shepherded waited trustfully for God's next move.

Many Christian artists throughout history have expressed this moment in various media. My favorite is the fresco painting called the *Liberation of Saint Peter* by the Renaissance artist Raphael. The artist created the scene in the apostolic palace of the Vatican. In the early sixteenth century, Raphael was painting a series of rooms at the same time Michelangelo was painting his Sistine Chapel a short distance away. The rooms of Raphael as well as the Sistine Chapel are part of the Vatican Museum today.

The fresco consists of three scenes in symmetrical balance. In the center, the angel of freedom awakens Peter in his cell. The barred cell is on an upper level, reached by steps to the left and right. On the right side, the angel guides the stunned and still-drowsy Peter past the sleeping guards. On the left side, one guard has noticed the light generated by the angel and awakens his bewildered companion, pointing to the miraculously illumined cell. The scene is a celebration of light. The angel casts a transcendent and radiant light into the scene, while the light of the moon and the crack of dawn spread their more subtle glow. The reflections off the armor and the prison walls create an extraordinary effect.

Art historians say that Raphael gave Peter the facial features of Pope Julius II, who commissioned the work. He intended it to express the freedom that God gives to the church in the face of overwhelming odds. The power of Christ's resurrection is made evident in its divine liberation from all the powers of evil and oppression. Certainly we are all imprisoned in our own waywardness and ensnared in the sin of the world. Every viewer of Raphael's masterpiece can be led to contemplate the amazing grace that freed us when we were lost in darkness without an exit sign in sight.

Early tradition maintains that the chains of Peter from the prison cell were kept in Jerusalem, where they were venerated by Christian pilgrims. In the fourth century, the patriarch of Jerusalem presented the chains to Aelia Eudoxia, the wife of the eastern emperor Theodosius II, and she brought them to Constantinople. Later, she sent a portion of the chains to Rome with her daughter Licinia Eudoxia, the wife of the western emperor Valentinian III, who gave them to Pope Leo I. It seems that another set of chains was already venerated in Rome, the fetters in which Peter was bound when he was imprisoned later by Nero in the capital city. In the fifth century, the Church of St. Peter in Chains was built in Rome to venerate these relics. Today these chains are kept in a large reliquary and may be seen under the main altar of the basilica.

The fallen chains and the freedom given to Peter launch a new phase in his ministry to the church. When Peter comes at dawn to the house where many of the disciples were staying, and when they finally let him into the house, their first impulse must have been to cry out with joyful surprise. But Peter motions for them to keep quiet. He did not want them to awaken the neighborhood and betray his presence. He quickly tells them how the angel delivered him, and he asks them to tell James and the other believers what has happened. This James was the one called the brother of Jesus, not the apostle who had recently been executed. James will become the leading figure of the church in Jerusalem after the departure of Peter.

Peter then departs from the house, and as the text of Acts says, "went to another place" (Acts 12:17). The escalating persecution and the desire of city authorities to kill Peter explains why Peter left his leadership position in the Jerusalem church and went to another place. All available evidence indicates that, at this point, he becomes a traveling missionary in other parts of the world. By freeing Peter from his prison in Jerusalem, God has liberated Peter to minister in other lands. No longer is Peter's fishing for men and women limited to the regions of Galilee and Judea. He will become a universal shepherd and care for God's scattered flock.

Peter Travels to Antioch and Beyond

To gain a better understanding of Peter's apostolic journeys, we depend on the letters of Paul and Peter, historical writings, and other early traditions. In Paul's letter to the Galatians, he reveals a great deal about his relationship with Peter. He first describes his initial meeting with Peter in Jerusalem, three years after Paul's Damascus Road conversion experience (Galatians 1:18). At that encounter, Paul learns directly from Peter about the events of Christ's life and his relationship with the apostles. Paul then describes another meeting fourteen years later in which he and his companion Barnabas went up to Jerusalem. There he met with Peter, James, and John, receiving from them supportive encouragement for his mission to the Gentiles.

> On the contrary, when they saw that I had been entrusted with the gospel for the uncircumcised, just as Peter had been entrusted with the gospel for the circumcised (for he who worked through Peter making him an apostle to the circumcised also worked through me in sending me to the Gentiles), and when James and Cephas and John, who were acknowledged pillars, recognized the grace that had been given to me, they gave to Barnabas and me the right hand of fellowship, agreeing that we should go to the Gentiles and they to the circumcised. (Galatians 2:7–9)

Paul takes seriously the reputation of these three "pillars" of the church: James, John, and Peter, who is here called by his Aramaic name, Cephas. Paul wants to meet with them to get their assessment of his work among the Gentiles. The three pillars acknowledged God's grace working within his mission and endorse his work. Paul affirms that both he and Peter are missionary apostles: Paul entrusted with evangelizing the "uncircumcised," the Gentiles, and Peter entrusted to the circumcised, the Jews.

This division of labor between Peter and Paul, while it expresses a general complementarity between the missions of the two apostles, was not workable in practice, especially outside of Judea. Because in most places the population was mixed, any precise division into two missionary areas was unattainable. Peter certainly had ministered among Gentiles, and Paul preached to both Jews and Gentiles during his travels.

It is difficult for us to imagine today the problems resulting from the early church's efforts to include Jews and Gentiles together.

Christianity, in its earliest years, was not a separate religion, but a form of messianic Judaism. So Jewish Christians who believed in Jesus as the Messiah continued to live their ancient faith as Jews, which included covenant markers such as circumcision, dietary practices, and purity regulations. And when Gentiles began to become believers, most Jewish Christians assumed that Gentiles would practice these covenant traditions of their sacred history.

Paul was the missionary proclaiming to the Gentiles that receiving the gospel did not include taking on these Jewish practices. People are made right before God not through what they themselves accomplish but through what Jesus Christ has done. As Paul wrote in this timeless statement, "A person is justified not by the works of the law but through faith in Jesus Christ" (Galatians 2:16). By joining oneself to Jesus, living "in Christ," a person achieves what the covenant regulations accomplish and much more. So Paul dispensed with all such covenant markers in his evangelizing of the Gentiles. It seems that Peter completely agreed with Paul's approach in his mission to the Gentiles. After all, it was Peter who baptized Cornelius, the first Gentile to be received into the church.

However, Paul describes in his letter a strong disagreement he had with Peter while they were both ministering to the church in the city of Antioch. It seems that Peter traveled to Antioch after leaving Jerusalem and spent an extended amount of time there. Antioch was the third largest city of the empire, after Rome and Alexandria, and consisted of a mixed population of Jews and Gentiles. Large numbers converted to the faith, making Antioch the most important city for the early expansion of the church. Luke tells us that here the followers of Jesus were called "Christians" for the first time.[5]

Paul accused Peter of hypocrisy when he withdrew from table fellowship with Gentiles. He had regularly eaten with Gentiles in

Antioch, but only when Jewish Christians sent by James came from Jerusalem did he withdraw. This is how Paul narrates the event.

> When Cephas came to Antioch, I opposed him to his face, because he stood self-condemned; for until certain people came from James, he used to eat with the Gentiles. But after they came, he drew back and kept himself separate for fear of the circumcision faction. And the other Jews joined him in this hypocrisy, so that even Barnabas was led astray by their hypocrisy. But when I saw that they were not acting consistently with the truth of the gospel, I said to Cephas before them all, "If you, though a Jew, live like a Gentile and not like a Jew, how can you compel the Gentiles to live like Jews?" (Galatians 2:11–14)

The Jewish Christians of Jerusalem, backed by James, upheld the Jewish sacred practices. Some thought that all believers should first become Jews; others thought that certainly Jewish Christians, like Peter, should maintain the precepts of the Torah. Because Peter had agreed with Paul in principle that the Gentiles were freed from following the covenant regulations, Paul declared Peter's actions inconsistent with his beliefs and accused him of compromising the freedom that the Gentiles had been given in Christ.

There is a wide range of opinion on the seriousness and the length of this rift between Peter and Paul. Some consider this an example of two strong personalities clashing over an important issue that was soon resolved. Others deduce that the conflict led to a prolonged divide between the two.[6] The problem, of course, is that the letter gives us only Paul's point of view. We are not given Peter's perspective on the wide range of issues involved with Jewish and Gentile converts in a mixed community.

As apostle to the Jews, Peter knew that many Jewish believers in Jesus continued to demonstrate loyalty to the covenant laws and ancestral customs that constituted their Jewish identity. Out of concern for his mission to the circumcised, he chose to honor the deeply felt beliefs of his fellow Jews. The truth of the gospel, Peter felt, was not at stake. Paul, however, strongly disagreed. Although he clearly respected Peter's authority, Paul's passionate nature and strong belief in principles convinced him to challenge Peter for not "acting consistently with the truth of the gospel." By rebuking Peter publicly, he stood strongly for the basic principle of salvation through Jesus Christ and not through the Torah.

Paul believed that failing to stand resolutely on this principle would lead to division within the church. There would either be two churches separated by ethnicity, or the church would have a two-tiered membership with Gentile Christians occupying the lower tier. Such division would be a travesty for Paul, who wrote in the same letter, "There is no longer Jew or Greek, there is no longer slave or free, there is no longer male and female; for all of you are one in Christ Jesus" (Galatians 3:28). Paul judged that Peter was effectively rebuilding the very walls that Paul had torn down.

Although we don't know all the details, this confrontation between Peter and Paul demonstrates the challenges of pastoral leadership in the church. Often within communities there is a need to talk about differences, compromise over issues that are not essential, and make corrections where needed. The church must always seek unity within its necessary and important diversity. The ancient adage applies to many such situations: "In essentials unity, in doubtful things liberty, but in all things charity."

In the tug-of-war between principle and pragmatism, Peter seems to have taken a middle way. He tried to hold both sides at once: the party of James in Jerusalem and the followers of Paul. Essentially he agreed with Paul, that covenant markers were not essential practice for believers, neither Jewish nor Gentile. But for the sake of peace and for the unity of the church, Peter stepped back from table fellowship so as not to create problems for the Jewish Christians and their relationship with the church in Jerusalem.

Peter's concern was for the unity of the church. There are indicators throughout the New Testament that Peter was the one most responsible for holding together the Christian communities throughout the Roman Empire that were in many ways so different from one another. Considering the many conflicts and tensions within the early churches, it is remarkable that they did not break apart into various splinter groups.

Unlike Paul, who was continually going to the fringes to establish new churches, it seems that Peter focused his pastoral activity on visiting those churches already established to encourage their faith and unity in Christ. These complementary aspects of evangelization are both essential for witnessing God's kingdom in the world. To use a metaphor from physics, Peter represents the centripetal force, moving in a curved path toward the center, and Paul represents the centrifugal force, moving away from the center. On the one hand, Peter worked to preserve the unity of the church, holding together the divergent positions of James and Paul, and expressing the rock-solid foundation of the community. Paul, on the other hand, moved outward to spread the gospel to the whole world, breaking boundaries, pushing the church to the fringes, and seeking to remove the barriers that divided people from one another and from God.[7]

Without the unifying force of Peter, Paul's mission would become scattered, forever in danger of dissolution. And without the energy of Paul, Peter's mission would be in danger of becoming stagnant, too attached to the status quo. The church must always move out into the world, and at the same time it must always be drawing people inward with open arms and embracing them as the universal family of God.

The Apostolic Council in Jerusalem

Many years after Peter's departure from Jerusalem following his escape from prison, he returned to the city for an important gathering of church leaders. This final episode of Peter in the book of Acts is often called a council, the prototype of later church councils called to settle particularly troublesome controversies and to unify the church in its mission. The issue in question here was a perennial one for the early church—the inclusion of Gentiles. The debate was not whether Gentiles should be received into the church—that decision had been made long before—but on what basis they should be included. The key question that needed a final resolution was whether Gentiles must become Jewish to be genuinely Christian.

The controversy had incited much dissension within the local churches spread throughout the empire, and so Paul and Barnabas were appointed to go up to Jerusalem to discuss this issue with the apostles and elders of the mother church. This matter was too important to be left to local debate, and it must be a decision for the whole church. A definitive, churchwide resolution was essential for the church's ongoing mission.

After considerable debate among the apostles and elders, Peter stands to speak:

> My brothers, you know that in the early days God made a choice among you, that I should be the one through whom the Gentiles would hear the message of the good news and become believers. And God, who knows the human heart, testified to them by giving them the Holy Spirit, just as he did to us; and in cleansing their hearts by faith he has made no distinction between them and us. Now therefore why are you putting God to the test by placing on the neck of the disciples a yoke that neither our ancestors nor we have been able to bear? On the contrary, we believe that we will be saved through the grace of the Lord Jesus, just as they will. (Acts 15:7–11)

Peter places the emphasis on God's initiative, as he reviews his experience with the household of Cornelius. He observes that God selected him to be the one through whom the Gentiles would hear the good news and become believers in Jesus Christ. He then stresses that God gave the Holy Spirit to these Gentiles just as the Spirit had been given to Jewish believers at Pentecost. In terms of access to salvation, there is no distinction between Jews and Gentiles.

Peter's statement dovetails with the views of Paul and Barnabas. Because it is God who purifies the hearts of both Jews and Gentiles through faith, the church should put no unnecessary obstacle in the way to salvation. Peter's conclusion states the principle at the heart of the council's pronouncement: both Jews and Gentiles will be saved through the grace of the Lord Jesus.

The final witness at the council is James, who became the leader of the church in Jerusalem after Peter's departure. He shows deep respect for the stature of Peter and reaffirms the pivotal role of Peter in opening the door of the kingdom to Gentiles. He reinforces Peter's testimony by linking it to the ancient prophets. He quotes a passage from Amos to show that the restored kingdom of Israel will include people of all nations, "so that all other peoples may seek the Lord—even the Gentiles over whom [God's] name has been called" (Acts 15:17).

In a remarkable display of unity, the council issues its teaching and sends it to the local churches spread throughout the world. It demonstrates the work of the Holy Spirit in a momentous time of decision for the whole church. It shows that the work of the Holy Spirit is both conservative, safeguarding the teachings of Jesus and the ancient Scriptures, and progressive, bringing new understanding in every age of history.

Although Peter leaves the stage of Acts after this episode, the remainder of the book completes the story of the church's growth from Jerusalem to Rome. Through the mission of both Peter and Paul, the church shows itself to be the instrument of salvation in bringing people of every nation to Christ.

Questions for Reflection and Group Discussion

1. By freeing Peter from his prison in Jerusalem, God liberates Peter to minister in other lands. Why does the church often experience new life as a result of persecution?

2. Peter was freed from prison because he responded to God's lead. In what aspect of your life might you admit your own powerlessness and surrender to God to show you the way?

3. How does the disagreement between Peter and Paul in Antioch demonstrate the wisdom of the saying: "In essentials unity, in doubtful things liberty, but in all things charity"?

4. In what sense were the missions of Peter and Paul complementary within the early church? Why are both the Petrine and Pauline dynamism essential for the church today?

5. How does the apostolic council in Jerusalem demonstrate both authoritative and collaborative leadership in the early church? What are the lessons from this council for the church today?

11

Peter Serves the Church
in Rome

The spread of the gospel of Jesus Christ from Jerusalem to Rome has fascinated and inspired Christians from the earliest times. Jerusalem, the place from which the good news was launched to the world at the command of the risen Lord, bore the weight of Roman rule in the eastern parts of the empire. The emperor expected only two things from those who ruled in his name: to collect taxes and keep the peace. The rebellion of the Jewish people against their Roman oppressors prevented these imperial expectations from being met, especially when the emperors demanded to be honored as deities and worshipped with sacrifice. The great Jewish revolt of AD 66 provoked the emperor to order the siege of Jerusalem. By AD 70, in an orgy of bloody violence, the city and its temple were completely destroyed.

While the path from Rome to Jerusalem resulted in oppression and destruction, the way from Jerusalem to Rome created much different results. Rome ruled over the vast territory of what is today Israel-Palestine, Syria, Turkey, Greece, Egypt, northern Africa, and western Europe. Thanks to the Roman system of roads and free passage, the good news of the Jewish Messiah was brought from Jerusalem to the four corners of the empire. The Jewish synagogues throughout the empire provided the original outposts from which the gospel was preached and the people evangelized. By the early AD 40s, the gospel had reached the imperial city of Rome and the first house churches had begun forming there. The capital of the empire had been infiltrated by the gospel.

The book of Daniel prophesied that four earthly kingdoms would rule over the Jewish people, culminating in the fourth kingdom, the Roman Empire, represented by a terrible beast. This Roman beast, according to Daniel's visions, will blaspheme the Most High and persecute God's holy ones (Daniel 7:25). But in the days to come, the prophet proclaimed, God will "set up a kingdom that shall never be destroyed" (Daniel 2:44). The Son of Man will receive this kingdom from God and will be given everlasting "dominion and glory and kingship," being served by all "peoples, nations, and languages" (Daniel 7:14). The Jewish people understood these prophetic texts as referring to the time of the Messiah, and Jewish Christians understood them to refer to the kingdom of God, established by Jesus Christ.

As Christian missionaries came to Rome, the destructive powers of the empire slowly began to be undermined by the gospel of peace and justice. The persecution experienced by believers at the hands of the Romans would only further the growth of God's messianic kingdom in the world. Of course, this kingdom of God was only in the form of a small mustard seed when the gospel reached Rome in the AD 40s; it would require two more centuries of steady growth before being officially acknowledged by the rulers of the empire. Yet, slowly but surely, the teachings of the apostles, the charity of the community, the breaking of the bread, and the prayers of God's holy ones would infiltrate the city so that Jesus would be acknowledged as the King of kings and the true ruler of all of the nations.

Jesus had introduced Peter to the powers of the Roman Empire at Caesarea Philippi. The city was dominated by a massive wall of rock and a temple in which to honor the emperor with sacrifices. Nowhere else in Palestine was the authority of Rome more clearly expressed. Jesus chose this place to proclaim Peter as the indestructible rock on which the church would be built, and to give him the royal keys of authority in God's kingdom. Here, Jesus connected the mission of Peter with the power of Rome and the keys of God's kingdom with the authority of the empire. While Jesus assured Peter that the church would not be overcome by the powers of the underworld and that God's kingdom would be everlasting, the days of Rome and its powerful empire were numbered and its destructive might would be overcome.

Jesus knew, of course, that this would not be Peter's last encounter with the power of Rome. Peter's missionary travels would extend through many areas of the empire, and his leadership would culminate in its capital. As a witness to Christ from Jerusalem to Rome, Peter was God's primary instrument in transforming the fourth kingdom of Daniel's prophecy into the geographical center of the growing church.

Although we have far less information about Peter's travels than we do about Paul's, we must assume that Peter was a successful missionary organizer and preacher. We know that he was committed to the church's mission extending out to the world. But his concern was not only the church's expansion but also the development and unity of the many and diverse churches extending across the empire from Jerusalem to Rome.

Whether Peter first came to Rome early in his pastoral career in the AD 40s or closer to his martyrdom in the 60s, we don't know. After Peter's imprisonment and miraculous release in Jerusalem, Acts tells us that Peter "left and went to another place" (Acts 12:17). But it is impossible to know for sure where Peter traveled next. One tradition claims that Peter went immediately to Rome and there became the bishop of the church for twenty-five years until his martyrdom. Other sources indicate that Peter traveled elsewhere, including extended stays in Antioch, Corinth, and Asia Minor.

Peter's stature and influence throughout the church, whether he was a traveling missionary or the more stationary leader of the church in Rome, must have been considerable. His role at the apostolic council in Jerusalem, where he returned after having left the city for many years, indicates his continuing importance. When Peter became leader of the church in Rome, whether earlier or later, his authority became most assured. The word of the Gospels about Peter—as the rock of Christ's church given the keys of authority (Matthew 16:18–19), as the faithful one who will return to strengthen his brothers (Luke 22:32), and as the one Jesus commissioned to feed his flock (John 21:15)—cannot apply only to the earliest period of the church. They describe Peter's entire ministerial life up to and including his martyrdom in Rome.

Peter Writes to the Exiles of the Dispersion

The first letter of Peter is an encyclical from Rome addressed to Christian house churches in five Roman provinces of Asia Minor (present-day Turkey). It was sent to be circulated among these communities, meant to be read at Eucharist on the Lord's Day, and designed to build up the faith of its hearers during times of trial.

> Peter, an apostle of Jesus Christ,
> To the exiles of the Dispersion in Pontus, Galatia, Cappadocia, Asia, and Bithynia, who have been chosen and destined by God the Father and sanctified by the Spirit to be obedient to Jesus Christ and to be sprinkled with his blood:
> May grace and peace be yours in abundance. (1 Peter 1:1–2)

What is the relationship between Peter and the Christians in these five provinces? The most common view is that these are churches Peter visited during his missionary journeys before he went to Rome. Now Peter is writing from Rome to offer encouragement to these Christians in their struggles. He addresses them as "exiles of the Dispersion," in the metaphorical sense that all people are exiles in the world because our true home is with God.

An alternative theory holds that the people of these five provinces became Christians in Rome and were then expelled by the emperor into these distant territories.[8] They were some of those Jews and Jewish Christians deported from Rome in AD 49 by the emperor Claudius (referred to in Acts 18:2). The emperor relocated them to strategically located colonial areas in Asia Minor in order to expand and strengthen the empire. The recipients of Peter's letter are then literally "aliens and exiles" (1 Peter 2:11) in a distant and foreign land.

Although Peter's authorship of this letter was unchallenged throughout the history of the church, some modern scholars attribute the authorship to someone other than Peter. Objecting that the Greek style and theology is too developed for a simple Jewish fisherman from Galilee, they propose that the letter was attributed to Peter to give it authority. I maintain, however, that the best arguments lie on the side of the traditional view of Petrine authorship.

First, as we mentioned when discussing Peter's origins in Galilee, his hometown of Bethsaida was heavily Greek-speaking, although he later moved to Aramaic-speaking Capernaum. Yet bilingual abilities would have helped Peter during the years he was building his fishing trade, and he would have further developed his skills after traveling through the Greek-speaking world for twenty to thirty years before writing this letter. Furthermore, studies of the language of 1 Peter indicate Semitic influences and suggest a Semitic author for whom Greek was a second language.

Second, although Peter undoubtedly developed into a more refined, bilingual speaker and possibly a writer, he could have been the author of the letter but not its writer. At the end of the letter, Peter states, "Through Silvanus, whom I consider a faithful brother, I have written this short letter" (1 Peter 5:12). This postscript could indicate that Silvanus, a frequent companion of Paul, helped to compose the letter for Peter.

Third, the letter alludes to the words and deeds of Jesus while Peter was present as well as moments from Peter's life during the ministry of Jesus. The letter has all the characteristics of one who was with Jesus and who personally witnessed his suffering and glory.

This first letter of Peter probably presents some of Peter's final correspondence before his death. It is a magnificent testimony of Peter's apostolic zeal to help the churches face the challenges of living in a hostile world. Although Peter does not directly state that he is writing from Rome, his final greetings imply that he writes from the capital city of the empire.

> Your sister church in Babylon, chosen together with you, sends you greetings; and so does my son Mark. Greet one another with a kiss of love. Peace to all of you who are in Christ. (1 Peter 5:13–14)

Babylon, almost all interpreters agree, is a code word for Rome. Just as Babylon was the archenemy of God's people during Judah's early history, so Rome is now the universal power that threatens Christ's church with destruction.

The letter is soaked with quotations, allusions, and images from the Hebrew Scriptures, demonstrating that Peter took seriously the importance of keeping Christianity within the framework of ancient Israel and ensuring that its Jewish character not be lost. Furthermore, the letter gives evidence that Peter reflected on the teachings, suffering, death, and resurrection of Jesus and pondered their meaning and significance for the infant church.[9]

Peter the Rock and Shepherd Addresses the Struggling Churches

Jesus helped Peter understand his mission by using images of a foundation rock and of a shepherd tending the flock. Now, in his letter to the churches, Peter uses similar images to help the early Christians understand their mission. And the words of Peter from Rome also speak across the centuries to us who desire to serve Christ's church today.

Peter the Rock uses the picture of a stone to reflect on Christ and his relationship to the church. He uses quotations from the psalms and prophets that describe Christ as a rejected stone, a stumbling stone, and a cornerstone. According to God's grand design for the church, we are "like living stones" being built upon the foundation stone of Jesus into a spiritual house.

> Come to him, a living stone, though rejected by mortals yet chosen and precious in God's sight, and like living stones, let yourselves be built into a spiritual house, to be a holy priesthood, to offer spiritual sacrifices acceptable to God through Jesus Christ. (1 Peter 2:4–5)

As individual believers are built up in faith, each one becomes an integral part of God's house, according to the divine architectural plan. This holy temple exists for the singular purpose of worshiping God. In contrast to the temple in ancient Israel, made of lifeless stones, this spiritual house is made of living stones. Rather than an inherited priesthood made up only of Levites, all Christians form a holy priesthood. Instead of material sacrifices, Christians offer spiritual sacrifices of prayer and praise, of self-consecration and self-giving. Such sacrifices are acceptable to God not on account of the one offering them but because they are made "through Jesus Christ," that is, joined with his perfect sacrifice and united with his Spirit.

While Peter the Rock refers to Jesus as the cornerstone and his church as the living stones of God's temple, Peter the Shepherd refers to Jesus as "the chief shepherd" and understands his own leadership within the church as modeled on the life of Jesus.

> Now as an elder myself and a witness of the sufferings of Christ, as well as one who shares in the glory to be revealed, I exhort the elders among you to tend the flock of God that is in your charge, exercising the oversight, not under compulsion but willingly, as God would have you do it—not for sordid gain but eagerly. Do not lord it over those in your charge, but be examples to the flock. And when the chief shepherd appears, you will win the crown of glory that never fades away. (1 Peter 5:1–4)

By the time Peter wrote this letter from Rome, Jesus' lakeside charge to him, "Tend my sheep," had been fulfilled for several decades through Peter's pastoral care of the church in many areas of the world. Peter's apostolic exhortation, "Tend the flock of God that is in your charge," reflects his own experience of suffering and joy among God's flock and serves as a kind of final testament to his successors.

In offering his pastoral advice, Peter reminds the elders that they do not own the flock; rather, they exercise "oversight" of God's flock. He describes the kind of leadership they should exercise with a series of contrasts. They should shepherd the community not under compulsion but willingly, not inspired by greed but by a desire for service, and not lording it over them but by being "examples to the flock." The image of Christ the Shepherd must encourage them to act like shepherds toward all entrusted to their care.

Peter's letter shows the strong bonds that joined the early communities of the church stretched across the world. From the church in Rome, Peter reached out to the small towns in the remote provinces of Asia Minor. He reminded them that they were not alone but part of a worldwide church united together in suffering and in hope. The struggles of believers are necessary for following in the steps of Christ, and they are part of the transformation through which evil will be overcome and through which believers will share in God's eternal glory in Christ.

Mark's Gospel as the Memoirs of Peter

At the end of his letter, Peter sends greetings from "my son Mark." This is an affectionate reference to John Mark, known from Acts and Paul's letters. It was to the home of Mark's mother, Mary, in Jerusalem that Peter had fled many years before after his miraculous escape from prison (Acts 12:12). John Mark must have remembered this highly charged moment for the rest of his life. Peter could not have known on the night he left Jerusalem that decades later his life would be interwoven again with that of Mark, Mary's wide-eyed son.

Mark became Peter's disciple and interpreter in Rome. By now an experienced and wiser man, he must have spent countless hours listening to Peter teach about Jesus based on his personal experiences with him. Mark surely asked Peter many questions to help him understand who Jesus was and what it meant to follow him. Then, according to Papias, writing at about the turn of the second century, Mark based his Gospel on what he had learned from the teachings of Peter: "Mark having become the interpreter of Peter, wrote down accurately whatever he remembered of the things said and done by the Lord, but not however in order."[10]

Either shortly before or shortly after Peter's death, Mark edited Peter's memoirs of Jesus into the Gospel according to Mark.[11] Faced with growing Roman persecution and the tragic deaths of church leaders, it became increasingly necessary for someone to preserve in writing the teachings and events of the life of Jesus, and with these words to encourage Christians suffering persecution. Mark seemed to be the ideal person for this task because he had grown up in the first Christian community in Jerusalem, had traveled and worked with Peter and Paul, and had the literary skills to accomplish this.

It is well recognized that Mark's Gospel was the first of the four; hence, before this book no literary form called a "gospel" existed. Mark not only wrote down the words and deeds of Jesus according to the memoirs of Peter, he also created a whole new literary form. Mark opened his work with these words: "The beginning of the good news of Jesus Christ, the Son of God." *Euangelion* is the Greek word for "good news" used here. It can also mean "glad tidings" or simply "gospel."

As Mark's writing demonstrates, a Gospel is more than a biography. Rather than offering a detailed and chronological description of Jesus' life, Mark selected certain moments of Jesus' life that particularly described his words and deeds as good news for the audience to which Mark was writing. Rather than describe Jesus' family, his education, and his young adulthood, Mark began with the public ministry of Jesus in Galilee, pointing to those crucial moments that portrayed Jesus as the Messiah and Son of God. Although Mark had many sources for the material of his Gospel, Peter seems to be his most important and consistent source of information. Peter not only provided Mark with his own memories, but helped Mark to shape his narrative into a font of hope for all who would hear it.

In his Gospel, Mark narrated the events of Jesus' life and also taught others how to be disciples of Jesus. He used the lives of the historical disciples to show people in his own generation how to follow in the way of Jesus. Mark gave examples of good discipleship and also provided many illustrations of failure in discipleship. For these demonstrations, Peter was a prime inspiration and became Mark's representative figure for Christian discipleship. Through Peter, Mark portrays the role of the disciple as one who struggles and fails, learns through his mistakes, and grows to become Jesus' outstanding follower and the leader of his church.

Mark composed his Gospel during the first serious persecution of the church. Under Nero, the Christians of Rome were undergoing great struggle. Many had seen their loved ones tortured and killed because they would not abandon their faith. Others were hounded by guilt for renouncing their faith to protect their families and survive another day. Mark developed his Gospel especially for these people. He used as a primary theme the idea that only through personal struggle and failure can disciples grow stronger in faith and in their understanding of Jesus. Of course, the primary character of the Gospel to exemplify this growth through weakness and failure was Peter the apostle. But Mark did not paint a negative portrait of Peter. Rather, he painted a human portrait, someone with whom his readers could easily identify. Through Mark's Gospel, Peter teaches us all how to gain courage and understanding by growing past our skepticism, narrow-mindedness, denials, and meltdowns. By slowly taking away the obstacles to God's grace working within him, Peter became the great fisherman of the church, the leader Jesus had called him to become.

As the first Gospel ever written, Mark's account became the primary source for Matthew and Luke. These writers took the basic frame of Mark's Gospel and added material from their own sources, arranging the narrative in a way that would be most impactful for the communities to whom they wrote. In these other Gospels, too, Peter is the primary character and model of discipleship. Therefore, we can state that Peter is one of the three primary authorities behind the writings of the New Testament. He is the prime influence for the synoptic Gospels (Matthew, Mark, and Luke), just as Paul is the principle source of the thirteen Pauline letters, and John is the authority behind the Gospel of John, the Johannine letters, and Revelation.

Peter's Final Imprisonment in Rome

Near the Church of St. Peter in Chains, the church containing the relics of Peter's prison chains from both Jerusalem and Rome, stands the Mamertine Prison. It can be found on the slope of the Capitoline Hill close to the Roman Forum. The ancient Romans simply called the site *carcer* (Latin for "prison"), since it was the only prison in the ancient city and was reserved for significant criminals of the state. Incarceration was a temporary measure, with the prison serving as a holding cell prior to execution. The prison dates to the seventh century BC and is mentioned by several classical writers, one of whom says "neglect, darkness, and stench make it hideous and fearsome to behold."

The prison remained in use until at least the fourth century AD, when it became a pilgrimage site. Although there are no historical accounts of Peter being held here, the tradition of Peter's captivity here before his death in Nero's circus on Vatican Hill had taken hold by the fifth century. The site continues to attract pilgrims today.

The Mamertine Prison consists of two vaulted chambers, one above the other. The upper room is on a level that was the ground level of the prison in ancient times. The walls are made of blocks of tufa on which is mounted a plaque engraved with the names of the prison's most celebrated prisoners. At the back is a small altar with busts of both Saint Peter and Saint Paul, whose imprisonment before their martyrdom is remembered here. The lower room was originally accessed through a round opening in the floor of the upper room. The condemned prisoners were thrown down or lowered through a hole to await their gruesome fate. The hole is now covered with a grate, and the lower floor is accessed by a modern staircase.

This lower cell, which was originally a cistern to catch water from a spring in the rock, today contains an altar and a relief of Peter baptizing his fellow prisoners. To the left of the altar is a column to which

Peter was tied and from which he is said to have converted his guards to Christianity. In the floor in front of the altar is a round opening leading to the spring, the water from which Peter baptized the prisoners and guards. On the front of the altar, standing out against a red marble background is the upside-down cross of Peter, a reminder that he was crucified feet up and head to the ground at his own request, because he did not consider himself worthy to die in the same manner as his Lord.

The dark and hideous prison has been transformed into a place where pilgrims may reflect on Peter and the early martyrs of the church. Although Peter was not miraculously released from this prison by an angel of God, his witness unshackled countless believers from the fear of despair. From his stone cell, Peter served his final hours as rock of the church, teaching anyone who would listen in that dank jail about the liberating Christ and the hope of God's kingdom.

The Inverted Cross on Vatican Hill

The Basilica of Santa Maria del Popolo dominates the monumental piazza welcoming pilgrims as they enter the city of Rome from the north. And within this church is one of the greatest paintings of the Baroque era—the Crucifixion of Saint Peter. The painter, known as Caravaggio, after the northern Italian town where he was born, created this work to illustrate the moment when Peter was crucified in Nero's circus.

Here Peter is depicted not as a Herculean hero in the manner of Michelangelo, but as an old man suffering pain and fearing death. The black, impenetrable background accentuates the four sharply illuminated figures of the scene. Peter and his three executioners create a cross of bodies as rope, muscles, and brute strength struggle to raise Peter on his cross. The three carry out their assigned task efficiently and anonymously. Their faces hidden or turned away, they are pushing, pulling, and dragging the cross to which Peter has been nailed by the feet with his head down. The grim ugliness of their movements convinces us that this is not a heroic drama but a miserable, shameful execution.

In this work, Caravaggio has turned on its head the baroque pomp of the papacy in his day. This painting was commissioned by the church in Rome to depict the death of its first bishop. Yet it is entirely drained of the kind of spiritual character we might expect from a treatment of this subject matter. The artist has chosen the moment when Peter's elderly but still-husky physique is raised in the most undignified position. His feet are above his head, and he is looking past the brutish nail that has been driven through his clenched left palm, perhaps to see the other Christians being executed with him.

The drama of the scene is understated; there is no bloodshed or sensationalism. Peter is neither angry, resisting, nor panicked. He is staunch, uncompromising, and resolute, the rock of faith on which the church would be secure. His face shows his resignation as he submits to Jesus' own prophecy about him: "When you were younger, you used to fasten your own belt and to go wherever you wished. But when you grow old, you will stretch out your hands, and someone else will fasten a belt around you and take you where you do not wish to go" (John 21:18).

The focus on these three figures and the absence of spectators transmutes the crucifixion of Peter from an historical event to a personal ordeal. The pulling, heaving, and straining of the savage executioners contrasts with Peter's acceptance of his martyrdom. They have significance only in relation to him. Their job is to hoist an old man up on a couple of crossed planks as quickly as possible. Who knows what the hourly rate might have been for this sort of sweaty toil in those days and how many others nearby awaited similar treatment. Their labor is the operative means through which Peter can glorify God and give witness to Jesus Christ.

Peter's inverted crucifixion in Nero's circus on Vatican Hill is the culmination of his years of preaching and evangelizing. Martyrdom is his final witness and the most glorious of all. The image of Peter, facing his death head-to-the-ground on a cross, endured through the ages in art and literature as a powerful statement about the nature of Christian faith. The same impulse that led the evangelists to portray Peter as a fallible and stumbling disciple during the life of Jesus also led artists to express his death in such an ignoble way. Peter is not the hero of the gospel; Jesus is. Peter is not the cornerstone of the church; Jesus is. Peter always points to Jesus, much as his comrade Paul does, who was also martyred by Nero. Paul affirms:

> [The Lord] said to me, "My grace is sufficient for you, for power is made perfect in weakness." So, I will boast all the more gladly of my weaknesses, so that the power of Christ may dwell in me. Therefore I am content with weaknesses, insults, hardships, persecutions, and calamities for the sake of Christ; for whenever I am weak, then I am strong. (2 Corinthians 12:9–10)

Questions for Reflection and Group Discussion

1. What were some of the consequences of bringing the gospel of Jesus Christ to the capital city of the Roman Empire? In what sense do these results continue today?

2. In his first letter, Peter describes the church as a temple made of "living stones" and "a holy priesthood" offering "spiritual sacrifices acceptable to God through Jesus Christ." How do these images influence your understanding of the church?

3. What are these "spiritual sacrifices" that we offer? How can they be "acceptable" to God?

4. When Peter, in his first letter, urges ministers in the church to "tend the flock of God" in their charge, what counsel does he offer to church leaders?

5. In what sense is Peter the authority behind the earliest written Gospels? In what ways does the writing of Mark's Gospel in Rome influence the Gospel's contents and its presentation of discipleship?

12

Peter as Bridge Builder and Universal Shepherd

At the closing liturgy of the Year of Faith, marking the fiftieth anniversary of the Second Vatican Council, Pope Francis presented the bones of Peter for public veneration. Eight bone fragments were nestled in an open bronze reliquary displayed for viewing to the side of the outdoor altar. While these represent only a small fraction of the bones encased below the papal altar at St. Peter's Basilica, this was the first time any of these precious relics have been exhibited at a liturgical ceremony since the earliest centuries of the church.

As the successor of Peter as the Bishop of Rome, Pope Francis blessed the bone fragments at the beginning of the Mass, and later he held the closed reliquary for several minutes in silent prayer while a choir sang the Nicene Creed. He did not mention the relics in his homily, but allowed these earthly remains of the apostle to once again lead the faithful to Jesus. While no pope has ever declared the bones to be authentic, Paul VI came cautiously close in 1968 when he announced the following: "New analyses—very patient and very detailed—have been made, which led to results which, relying upon the opinion of competent and careful experts, we think positive: the relics of Saint Peter have been identified in a way which we consider as persuasive."[12]

For many people the bones are a source of speculation and intrigue. For the faithful, they are a profound symbol and speak more loudly than words of the solidity and continuity of the church, founded by Jesus Christ and built upon Peter the Apostle. In a world spiraling into confusion and seeking a solid rock upon which to stand, these precious relics represent hope in the promises of Christ.

Buried on the Side of Vatican Hill

Neither Jews nor Christians were popular in imperial Rome, largely due to their abhorrence of the ancient Roman gods and their refusal to worship the emperor. In AD 64, a great fire devastated a large area of the city. When the people of the city started blaming the reigning emperor, the fanatical Nero, for the fire, suspecting him of wanting to rebuild the city according to his own grand plans, he deflected attention from himself by blaming the Christians. Because of rumors already circulating about this new religious group, they became an easy scapegoat. This began the first great period of Christian persecution in the empire.

Peter led the church in Rome during this difficult period. One famous story claims that when Nero's persecutions began, Peter was persuaded by the Christians of Rome to flee the city. While leaving along the Appian Way, he saw a vision of Jesus coming into the city. When Peter asked Jesus, "*Domine Quo Vadis?*" ("Where are you going, Lord?"), Jesus replied, "I am on my way to Rome to be crucified again." With that, Peter turned around, renewed with courage and resigned to face his ultimate ordeal. The Chapel of Domine Quo Vadis memorializes this story and serves to remind us all to follow through with our commitments and give honor to Christ with our entire life.

Peter was eventually killed in Nero's persecution somewhere between AD 64 and 68, when Nero himself died. He was executed in the circus, a long racetrack with bleachers that could accommodate thousands of spectators for horseraces and shows, which was on *Mons Vaticanus* ("Vatican Hill"). Here, according to early tradition, Peter was put to death by crucifixion, requesting to be executed upside down.

Outside the main part of the city of Rome and on the other side of the Tiber River, the area of the Vatican also contained a necropolis in which families would construct elaborate tombs to bury their dead. Condemned criminals did not have the right to a proper burial and were often left hanging on their crosses to serve as gruesome public warnings not to challenge Roman authority. However, either by bribery or by stealth, desiring to safeguard the remains of Peter, the Christians took his body and buried it in a simple grave in the area of the necropolis.

The great fire of Rome and the persecutions of Nero touched off an intermittent period of persecution of Christians that would last 250 years until Constantine legalized Christianity throughout the empire. But even during periods of extreme suffering, the church of Rome did not neglect the grave of Peter. Around AD 160, Christians erected a simple monument, a *tropaion*, over the grave.[13] Historians deduce that this was commissioned by Pope Anicetus, who reigned from AD 155 to 166. The shrine consisted of a marble tabletop supported by two marble columns and attached to a red plastered wall. A concave niche was carved into the wall behind the tabletop. The monument stood directly over the buried body of Peter. The memorial to Peter blended in with standard Roman architecture because Christian shrines were outlawed, but it marked for Christians the remains of their most venerated martyr.

During the next century, the red wall supporting the monument cracked, and a buttress was built to support the damaged wall. This buttress became known as the "graffiti wall" because through the years it has been covered in Christian notations and sayings in Latin and

Greek carved into the wall. When it was uncovered in the twentieth century, this additional construction was found to have become the most important element of the memorial to Peter.

In the year AD 313, the emperor Constantine granted toleration to the church and supplied the church in Rome with imperial funding for building churches. When building the first basilica to St. Peter, Constantine kept the second-century shrine over Peter's grave intact and encased it in a house of marble. He then built the basilica around it, with the tomb of Peter at its heart, directly under the high altar.

The building project required a drastic modification of the natural Vatican landscape. Vatican Hill was leveled, and the slope below Peter's grave was filled with dirt to create a level grade on which to build the church. This was the original Basilica of St. Peter, built before AD 333. In the sixth century, Pope Gregory the Great built an altar on top of the Constantinian one, and in the twelfth century, Pope Calixtus II added another altar over the earlier ones. The Old St. Peter's Basilica stood for over 1,200 years. The present-day basilica was begun at the beginning of the sixteenth century and wasn't completed until well into the next century. The present-day altar over the tomb was added by Pope Clement VIII (1592–1605).

Digging for the Bones of Peter

Pilgrims, popes, and builders through the centuries had always assumed that Peter was buried beneath the basilica. But because the vault containing Peter's grave had not been entered since the time of Constantine or before, no one was quite sure whether the bones of Peter were actually there. This all began to change in 1940, when Pope Pius XII decided to lower the floor of St. Peter's crypt in order to create more space for pilgrims and for the burial of future popes.

As workers dug beneath the floor, they found the ancient necropolis, which contained mostly pagan tombs and mausoleums. When the pope gave permission for formal excavations to begin, the digging eventually led toward the area beneath the high altar of St. Peter's.[14] But before reaching the area below the altar, the archeological team came upon their first Christian tomb. On one wall was a mosaic of Jonah falling from a ship and into the mouth of a huge fish. Another wall contained a mosaic of a fisherman who had caught a fish, while another fish swam away. And on the third wall, the mosaic depicted a shepherd carrying a sheep upon his shoulders.

Amazingly, each of these three images refers to Peter. Immediately before naming Peter as the Rock of his church, Jesus addressed him as "Simon son of Jonah!" (Matthew 16:17), and Peter's ministry to the Gentiles in Acts fulfills Jonah's call to preach to the Ninevites. At his calling, Jesus told Peter the fisherman that he would "fish for people" (Matthew 4:19). And finally, the risen Jesus exhorted Peter three times to be a shepherd when he commissioned him: "Tend my sheep" (John 21:15–17). After this intriguing discovery, the archeologists sought and received permission from Pope Pius XII to excavate under the high altar.

Digging beneath the several altars built over the ancient tomb of Peter, the excavators in time came upon the red plastered wall and the shrine built to honor the grave of Peter, as described by a writer in the second century. When they dug below the wall, the excited excavators uncovered about two hundred fifty fragments of bone. The team felt certain that they had found the very bones of Peter. Medical doctors confirmed that the skeletal fragments seemed to belong to a stoutly built male who had died in his late sixties. The pope ordered that the bones be sealed in lead boxes and stored in the papal apartments as World War II erupted.

Later studies on the bone fragments were disappointing. Dr. Venerando Correnti, an expert anthropologist commissioned to examine the fragments, concluded that there were three fibulas and six tibias, the bones of the lower leg of which human beings only have two each. His report concluded that there were three human skeletons present. Two were males who died in their fifties, and one was most probably a female who had died after the age of seventy. In addition, he reported that about a fifth of the fragments belonged to domesticated animals.

However, the story does not end there. During the excavation in about 1942, other bone fragments had been discovered. These were found in a cavity of the monument's buttressing wall, the so-called "graffiti wall." The bones had been marked and set aside among the archeological findings. When the remains found in the dirt under the monument were shown to be from a variety of sources, experts began to study the fragments from the buttress and the graffiti on the wall itself. The contents found in a marble-lined opening of this graffiti wall included 135 bone fragments, fragile pieces of cloth, and threads.

The Vatican hired Dr. Margherita Guarducci, a Greek inscription specialist from the University of Rome, to examine the shallow markings on the tombs in the area. In a mausoleum near Peter's tomb was a primitive scratched image of a bald and bearded elderly man, along with a faded inscription which she was able to read as follows: *PETRUS ROGA CHRISTUS JESU PRO SANCTIS HOMINIBUS CRESTIANUS AD CORPUS TUUM SEPULTIS* ("Peter pray Christ Jesus for the holy Christian men buried near your body.") When she began to inspect the graffiti wall, she found prayers and invocations for the dead as well as a kind of Christian code. For example, she realized that XP referred to Christ, AO designated Alpha and Omega, T symbolized the cross, MA denotes Mary, etc. She was also the first to discover references to Peter on the wall. The letter P with an E beneath it forms a key-shaped monogram designating the keeper of the keys of Christ's church.

Guarducci realized that this simple buttressing wall had become an object of great veneration. Most significantly, a broken piece of plaster was found in the wall's cavity bearing the Greek letters *PET ENI*, which she deduced could mark the place of Peter's remains: "Peter is in here." This kind of Christian cryptography was widely employed during the centuries of persecution. This coded language developed in response to the pressing need to keep certain beliefs hidden from hostile neighbors and Roman officials.

The same Dr. Correnti who had examined the bones buried under the red wall was now commissioned to examine the contents of the findings from the cavity in the graffiti wall. The findings indicated the decayed bones of one man along with the skeleton of a mouse. But, interestingly, the bones of the mouse were completely white, whereas the human bones were brown and dirty. The difference in color indicated that the bones of the man had once been buried in the ground, but the mouse had likely fallen into the cavity of the wall and died there. Furthermore, chemical analysis proved that the dirt on the man's bones matched the components in the dirt immediately under the monument to Peter. These bones had once, most probably, been buried in the grave of Peter.

Additional tests verify that the cloth fragments found with the bones had once been dyed purple. In addition, a few of the larger bones showed an unnatural reddish brown staining on their intact extremities, indicating that the bones had been wrapped in the purplish cloth. In fact it was the imperial purple, a dye extracted from Mediterranean Sea snails and kept under state control. And the threads woven into the cloth were of solid gold. Dr. Correnti concluded that the bones belonged to "a man of robust constitution," about five feet seven inches tall, between the age of sixty and seventy. The bone fragments were of one man, belonging to nearly every portion of his body.

If these are Peter's bones, then why had they been unearthed, wrapped in a cloth of purple and gold, and placed in the cavity of a supporting buttress? Perhaps they had been exhumed at some point in the second or third century to protect them during a period of persecution or foreign invasion. Or perhaps Constantine had ordered an excavation to satisfy his curiosity before encasing them in the floor of his new basilica. Either way, when the bones were returned, a hollow space was created in the buttressing wall, paneled with marble, filled with the bones wrapped in a splendid cloth, and sealed. This buttressing wall then became the most venerated part of the shrine to Peter, which accounts for its being covered in Christian graffiti, probably by devoted pilgrims.

There are two final notes to this account which are of interest to those of us following the footsteps of Peter to the end. First, it seems that the skull of Peter is not among the remains found in the wall, although a few cranial fragments were found. This fact conforms to an old tradition that the skulls of Peter and Paul are contained in a reliquary above the altar of Rome's cathedral, the Church of St. John Lateran. When Correnti was given permission to study the Lateran relics, his careful report concluded that nothing found in the reliquary of St. Peter at the Lateran interfered in any way with the claims made for the bones found in the graffiti wall.

Second, the bone fragments found belonged to every part of the human body except the feet. Human beings have twenty-six bones in each of their two feet. Yet not a single foot bone was found among the relics. This would be inexplicable except for the ancient tradition that Peter was crucified upside down, hanging from his feet nailed to the cross. Imagine how a brutal Roman soldier would remove the dead body of a man hanging from his feet on a cross. One whack at the ankles with an ax would quickly bring the body down. Evidently this is what happened to the body of Peter. The feet were lost when the vigilant Christians of Rome buried him in the simple tomb outside the circus of Nero.

So are these the bones of Peter? It is impossible to prove this definitely. The church is cautious about declaring this categorically and probably never will. However, it seems reasonable to believe this from a historical and archeological perspective, although there are many skeptics. And from the point of view of the early Christians, surely the remains of Peter would have been their most treasured relic and they would have wanted to preserve them at any price.

Pilgrims to Rome may receive permission in small groups to tour the Scavi (excavations) beneath St. Peter's Basilica. Every time I bring pilgrims here, I feel closer to Peter than anywhere else. As we make our way down through the damp chambers below the basilica, past the ancient funerary monuments that Constantine's workers covered with dirt before constructing the old St. Peter's Basilica, we walk the ancient streets that were walked by the first Christians of Rome. As we gradually approach the remains of the red wall, the graffiti wall, and the first shrine to Peter, I feel grateful for this courageous witness to Jesus Christ and the gift of his life for the church. The magnificent church above, built on the tomb of Peter, is a literal and physical memorial of the promise of Jesus to his disciples through the ages: "On this Rock I will build my church."

The Successors of Peter in Rome

The memorial shrine to Peter was constructed over his grave by one of the second-century popes named Anicetus (AD 155–66), desiring to give honor to his predecessor. At the same time, a nearby area of the grave complex was designated for the burial of future popes. The tombs excavated near that of Peter indicate a desire to be buried as close as possible to the tomb of Peter, and for the Roman bishops in the line of Peter, this would be a priority.

Another part of the second-century grave complex points to a room
entered from the alleyway directly behind the red wall. No burials were
found here, and the excavators could find no clear purpose for it. In
a corner of the room, a rectangular cistern had been built into the
ground. This reservoir could easily have held several people immersed
in water to the waist. Christian baptism could have been carried out
here, effectively screened from the eyes of hostile pagans.

The monument to Peter was not designed just to mark his grave.
It was the central focus of a walled-in courtyard, the floor of which
had been leveled and elegantly tiled. It could have accommodated a
hundred people within its boundaries. The table secured by the red
wall and supported by two columns seemed to fit into the other pagan
funerary monuments in order to hide its true purpose. But it seems
logical that it was also used as the table for celebrating the Christian Eucharist. It stood about six feet off the ground, but a few steps
and a platform below it would transform the whole area into Rome's
first church structure. If the complex served as a place for baptism and
Eucharist, then surely it was also utilized for the ordination of priests,
consecration of bishops, perhaps even marriages and funerals.

This sacred spot—centered on the relics of Peter, with its high altar,
walled-in area for worshippers, its baptistery, and cemetery for the
popes—anticipates in miniature the colossal building that today towers over its precious, underground ruins. Surely this hallowed ground
was revered by those who followed Peter as bishops of Rome and successors in his Petrine ministry for the church.

Linus is named in the ancient histories as the direct successor of
Peter in Rome. Irenaeus, in about AD 180, wrote: "The blessed apos-
tles, then, having founded and built up the church, committed into
the hands of Linus the office of the episcopate."[15] Jerome wrote that
Linus was "the first after Peter to be in charge of the Roman church."[16]
He began to shepherd the church in Rome during its first wave of

persecution, and it seems probable that it was Linus who presided over the burial of Peter at the Vatican Hill. At the end of his reign, Linus also died as a martyr. The *Roman Martyrology* states: "At Rome, Saint Linus, Pope and martyr, who governed the Roman church next after the blessed apostle Peter, was crowned with martyrdom and was buried on the Vatican Hill beside the same apostle."

The third pope and bishop of Rome was Anacletus (also called Cletus). Records indicate that he ordained twenty-five priests for the city of Rome, a signal that the Christian community in Rome had spread throughout the city by the close of the first century. Tradition holds that Anacletus, too, was buried alongside Peter and Linus.

Pope Clement, the fourth in succession, had previously been appointed by Peter to oversee the communication between the church of Rome and the other churches in cities throughout the empire.[17] He is remembered most for his epistle, one of the oldest Christian writings not included in the Scriptures. The letter refers to bishops (*episcopoi*), priests (*presbyteroi*), and deacons (*diakonoi*) ruling and serving the church. Clement wrote at the end of the apostolic age in which the threefold office—apostles, bishops-presbyters, and deacons—transformed to bishops, presbyters, and deacons. Clement stated that the apostles appointed bishops as successors and directed that these bishops should in turn appoint their own successors. He compared the liturgy of the new covenant with that of ancient Israel, pairing the threefold office of the church with the high priests, priests, and Levites who offered sacrifices in the temple of old.

When Clement was banished from Rome by the emperor Trajan and eventually martyred, he was succeeded in Rome by Pope Evaristus. Reigning at the turn of the second century, he was the first post-apostolic pope of the church, because the apostle John died just before or during his pontificate. Evaristus dealt with the rapidly growing Christian population of the city by appointing priests to titular churches, approving the priests as his delegates to celebrate the Eucharist and validating the churches as places of worship. In addition, he appointed seven deacons to assist him with his ministry to the city. Finally, his life was crowned with martyrdom and he was buried near the body of Peter.

These earliest popes, along with all the ones who followed, are honored today with mosaic medallions in the Roman Basilica of St. Paul Outside the Walls. The project was begun in the fifth century under the pontificate of Leo the Great, who planned to depict all the popes throughout history. The basilica has been destroyed several times, most recently by fire in 1823. The church was rebuilt in its original splendor and consecrated in 1855. Pope Pius IX restarted the project of creating medallions of each of the popes as they are elected. Today there are 267 medallions to the popes, from Peter to Francis, spanning the transepts and nave of the church. Each medallion has the pope's name in Latin and the dates of his papacy. The long display testifies in an extraordinary way to the endurance, continuity, and unity of the two-thousand-year-old church built on Peter.

As in the church's early years, so also today, the mission given by Jesus to Peter continues in the church. As the bishops succeed the apostles to carry on the apostolic mission that Jesus gave to his church, the bishop of Rome succeeds Peter to continue the specific ministry Jesus assigned to Peter among the apostles. As Peter held primacy among the twelve apostles, so the church in Rome and the authority of its bishop holds primacy among the communities throughout the world.

Irenaeus wrote of the "preeminent authority" of the church in Rome.[18] In the church's early centuries, Rome's vocation consisted in playing the part of arbiter, settling contentious issues by witnessing to the truth of the apostles' teaching. Irenaeus wrote, "If there are disputes within or among local churches, they should have recourse to the church in Rome, for there the tradition of the apostles is preserved." The church of Rome today continues to stand as the ecumenical center of unity for the universal church. The successor to Peter is the church's bridge builder, serving to establish and protect the unity of the church for which Jesus prayed. He is truly the rock on which the church is built, the one who strengthens his brother bishops, and the universal shepherd.

Back to Galilee and Beyond

The resurrection account of Matthew's Gospel begins with the journey of the women to the tomb at dawn. When they find the tomb open and empty, the angel of the Lord says to them, "Do not be afraid." Then the angel orders them to go and tell the disciples, "He has been raised from the dead, and indeed he is going ahead of you to Galilee; there you will see him" (Matthew 28:7). The women quickly depart, and on the way Jesus himself meets them and says: "Do not fear; go and tell my brothers to go to Galilee; there they will see me" (Matthew 28:10).

After the death of Jesus, Peter and the other disciples had scattered; their faith had crumbled and their hopes had died. But now the message of the women, incredible as it is, comes to them like a ray of light in the darkness. The women heard it twice, first from the angel and then from Jesus: "Go to Galilee; there they will see me."

Galilee is the place, for Peter, where it all began—the place where he was first called along the shores of the sea. Peter left his boat and nets and followed Jesus. Now, Galilee is the place of new beginnings. Here Peter can agree again to follow Jesus—but this time in light of all that he has learned about Jesus and about himself.

For those of us who have followed in the footsteps of Peter, returning to Galilee means starting again as well—rereading the Gospels in light of the cross and its victory. Like Peter, we listen to Jesus' call, witness his teachings and miracles, follow his journey to Jerusalem, watch the fear, denial, and betrayal of his disciples, and see with new eyes his passion and death on the cross. But this time as we read the Gospel again, we keep the end in mind. We experience anew Jesus' saving life in the assurance of his supreme act of love.

Our Galilee is the discovery of our personal encounter with Jesus Christ. It is the memory of his calling us, his look of mercy upon us, his invitation to follow him and to share in his mission. Our Galilee is recovering his challenging parables, his joyful teachings on the kingdom, his solidarity with our suffering, and our realization of his love for us.

Peter, as our elder brother, leads us to Galilee. He walks with us along the shore, rows the fishing boat for us on the sea, listens to Jesus with us, and shows us how to take up the call to follow. Then, with Peter, we can follow Jesus again to Jerusalem. This is the place of testing, of discipleship on trial, of learning humility through self-knowledge. Jerusalem is where, in agony and blood, the love of Jesus was demonstrated most convincingly.

Our journey to Jerusalem means learning to take up the cross, praying with Jesus that God's will be done, and sharing in his saving sacrifice through the Eucharist. With Peter to teach us through his own failures, we can return to the Upper Room, to the garden of prayer, to the place of denial, and to the place of Jesus' death and burial. In the light of his resurrection, we can learn again and again how to die to self and live for Christ, how to seek first his kingdom and depend on him for the rest, and how to follow him and share in his mission to the world.

Then, with Peter, we can leave Jerusalem and travel again to Rome, the place of witness. There Peter lived as a disciple of Jesus in the midst of a hostile empire. Our experience of Rome with Peter shows us what it means to give witness to Jesus in a world that does not welcome the gospel. Our Rome is living the Christian life with Spirit-empowered vigor, always ready to give others a reason for our hope. For us, Rome means walking with the flame of God's grace, allowing that flame to bring light and warmth to those who walk alone and in darkness.

Returning to Rome with Peter means realizing that we are part of a universal church, brothers and sisters with people from every land and culture, language and way of life. It means allowing ourselves to be embraced by that church as it extends its arms in welcome to saints and sinners alike. Rome is the place of mission, wherever in the world that might be for us. It is living under the guiding light of the Holy Spirit, filled with a gentle and humble joy, sent into the world to evangelize, bringing the good news of God's kingdom to those we meet along life's pilgrimage.

So, as wonderful as St. Peter's Basilica and its relics are, we do not leave our pilgrimage at a tomb. Rather, we take up the call of the risen Lord to go again to Galilee, to continue to follow in his way. If we don't understand the Peter of Galilee, we will not understand the Peter of Rome; for the fisherman of Galilee is the bishop of Rome. The blundering disciple is the same person who led the early church, preached the first sermon, worked the first miracle, baptized the first Gentiles, and was the primary witness to Christ.

Peter teaches us nothing greater than what it means to follow Jesus. He points the way to him and demonstrates what it means to travel in his footsteps. Peter's life was transformed through his relationship with Jesus, and walking with him as our model helps us desire to grow in discipleship. Peter shows that Jesus worked through Peter's many flaws to establish his church. Jesus works with us as well, allowing us to fail, get up again, and experience his forgiveness. With Peter, we walk our pilgrimage of life, always seeking to follow Jesus as his disciple. Let us be on our way!

Questions for Reflection and Group Discussion

1. Why are Peter's bones significant? What do they express to you about the nature of the church?

2. What seem to be some of the most convincing indications that the bones at the heart of the basilica are those of St. Peter himself?

3. In what sense is the bishop and church of Rome the center of unity for the universal church?

4. Why did the risen Jesus instruct Peter to go again to Galilee in order to encounter him? What does it mean for you to go again to Galilee with Peter?

5. What have you realized about Peter that makes him a companion and elder brother for you in your journey of faith?

Endnotes

1. James D. G. Dunn, *Unity and Diversity in the New Testament: An Inquiry into the Character of Earliest Christianity* (Philadelphia: Westminster Press, 1977).

2. Crossan and Reed, *Excavating Jesus: Beneath the Stones, Behind the Text* (San Francisco: HarperOne, 2001), 81–82.

3. Clement of Alexandria states that Peter had children, and that when Peter's wife was being led away to martyrdom, he followed her, comforting her, and urging her, "Remember thou the Lord." Another tradition states that the martyr St. Petronilla was Peter's daughter. On the strength of that tradition, her remains are today under the altar of St. Petronilla, which is just to the right of the Altar of the Chair in St. Peter's Basilica.

4. Pope Francis, Homily on the Feast of Pentecost, Vatican City, May 19, 2013.

5. See Acts 11:26—literally "followers of the Messiah." The term first distinguished disciples of Jesus from Jews, although it was not until early in the second century that Christians began to regularly use the term for self-designation.

6. See Martin Hengel, *Saint Peter: The Underestimated Apostle* (Grand Rapids: Eerdmans, 2010), 57–79. Hengel describes the clash between Peter and Paul as a protracted split with far-reaching consequences.

7. Stephen J. Binz, *Scripture: God's Handbook for Evangelizing Catholics* (Huntington, IN: Our Sunday Visitor Publishing, 2014), 135.

8. Karen H. Jobes, "1 Peter" in *Baker Exegetical Commentary on the New Testament* (Grand Rapids: Baker, 2005), 28–41.

9. 2 Peter is far more complex than 1 Peter for establishing a setting and time frame for the work. Commentators are divided on whether or not Peter had a hand in writing this work. Because the subject is more broad than this work warrants, I will refrain from commenting on 2 Peter and refer the reader to recent commentaries such as those by Richard J. Bauckham and Gene L. Green.

10. Papias, *Exegeses of the Logia of the Lord*, quoted by Eusebius of Caesarea, *Ecclesiastical History*, 3.39.15.

11. This is also the position of Irenaeus, Clement of Alexandria, Tertullian, Origin, and Jerome.

12. Thomas J. Craughwell, *St. Peter's Bones* (New York: Image, 2013), 105.

13. The Roman Gaius writing to the Phrygian Proclus, from Eusebius, *Ecclesiastical History* 2, 25, 6–7.

14. A fascinating account of the discovery of Peter's tomb can be found in John Evangelist Walsh, *The Bones of Saint Peter* (Manchester, NH: Sophia Institute Press, 2011).

15. Irenaeus, *Adversus Haereses* 3, 3, 3.

16. Jerome, *Chronicon* 14.

17. *Shepherd of Hermas* 8, 3, also *Liber Pontificalis.*

18. Irenaeus, *Adversus Haereses* 3, 3, 2.

About the Author

Stephen J. Binz is a biblical scholar, award-winning author, and popular speaker. Following graduate degrees from the Gregorian University and the Pontifical Biblical Institute in Rome and Jerusalem, Binz has developed Bible studies and offered numerous study trips and pilgrimages to biblical lands. His books have earned top awards from the Association of Catholic Publishers and the Catholic Press Association. He lives with his wife, Pamela, in Baton Rouge, LA. Information about his work may be found at www.Bridge-B.com.

Continue the Conversation

If you enjoyed this book, then connect with Loyola Press to continue the conversation, engage with other readers, and find out about new and upcoming books from your favorite spiritual writers.

Visit us at **LoyolaPress.com** to create an account and register for our newsletters.

Or scan the code on the left with your smartphone.

Connect with us through:

 Facebook
facebook.com
/loyolapress

 Twitter
twitter.com
/loyolapress

 **YouTube**
youtube.com
/loyolapress

Also Available

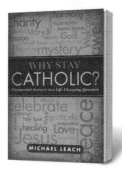

Why Stay Catholic?
Unexpected Answers to a
Life-Changing Question

MICHAEL LEACH
$14.95 • Paperback • 3537-5

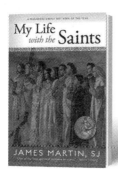

My Life with the Saints

JAMES MARTIN, SJ
$15.95 • Paperback • 2644-1

The Thorny Grace of It
And Other Essays for
Imperfect Catholics

BRIAN DOYLE
$14.95 • Paperback • 3906-9